UNSUCCEEDING

Waking Up from My American Dream

KYLE DRAKE

UNSUCCEEDING by Kyle H. Drake
Copyright © 2012 by Kyle H. Drake

Scripture quotations are from *The New American Standard Bible*®, copyright © 1960, 1962, 1963, 1968, 1971, 1972, 1973, 1975, 1977, 1995 by The Lockman Foundation. Used by permission.

Find more materials and give feedback on the book at:

www.unsucceeding.net

ISBN: 978-0-578-10182-8

Published in Atlanta, Georgia, USA by Jayebird Publishing

For my wife, Jaye,

who inspires me to be a better man

CONTENTS

FOREWORD

There's an old story about some people who, as a practical joke, slipped into a department store and changed all the price tags. The next day, some of the customers were overjoyed with the bargains while others were shocked by the grossly overpriced items.

Oscar Wilde once suggested that people know the price of everything but the value of nothing.

It's true. They do.

Me too.

Do you know why? Because everybody tells us the price and, in doing so, think they've defined value. The voices are everywhere and those voices are passionate. They come from the politicians, the preachers, the authors, the con artists and the "sellers of the trinkets," and they seem so sure. Then they remind us that we "only go around once," so we have to get it right the first time.

I'm old—as old as dirt—and over the years, I've listened to so many of those voices. It took me a long time to have an "attack of sanity" and to realize that those voices didn't know any more than I knew. Not only that, I found out that most of them were wrong. Late at night, an old man knows that sometimes he, as Mark Twain put it, "paid too much for his whistle."

Kyle Drake is a wise man with a wisdom that isn't his own. It's wisdom about forgiveness, value, and what's really important. As I read this book, I was affirmed in some choices I made when everybody told me I was a fool. But while I felt vindicated about some things, I also winced remembering the times I followed the crowd simply because I thought so many people couldn't be that wrong.

It's okay. Jesus is still quite fond of me and it could have been a whole lot worse.

Speaking of Jesus, his is the only voice that matters. Kyle Drake filters out the other voices and listens to the voice of the only One who knows the truth and, in fact, *is* the truth.

I know; it seems Jesus needed a course in leadership motivation. It seems everything he said was so counterintuitive. What's this about selling everything, denying oneself, washing feet, taking up crosses, and letting the dead bury their own dead? What does he mean by seeking first the kingdom of God and trusting that other things will be okay?

Jesus changed the price tags.

This is a fun book, but it's not comfortable. Like Jesus, it's counterintuitive. It will keep you up at night considering how much you've paid for your whistle. But like Jesus, there isn't condemnation here, or self-righteousness or manipulation. It is one man's honest and halting witness to the power of truth . . . a larger truth. *Unsucceeding* is one of those books that can change your life.

Henri Nouwen once wrote, "I am deeply convinced that the Christian leader of the future is called to be completely irrelevant and to stand in this world with nothing to offer but his or her own vulnerable self . . . The leaders of the future will be those who dare to claim their irrelevance in the contemporary world as a divine vocation" (Henri Nouwen, *In the Name of Jesus*).

It really is about Jesus.

It's hard to get the "irrelevant" part. But it is also the path toward incredible freedom and joy. It *is* about Jesus and once we see it, we discover that it's about us, too. It's about a love so pervasive that everything else pales in its light.

Steve Brown
Bible Teacher, Key Life Network; Professor, Reformed Theological Seminary, and author of *A Scandalous Freedom* and *Three Free Sins*

PROLOGUE

My life was perfect. On the surface it looked like a successful person's life. I didn't feel that I was any different from the next man who was successful at work and successful at home. In fact, I wasn't any different from the average guy who wanted to be good at his job, provide well for his family, and have a comfortable retirement. I was striving to be a well-rounded, reasonably successful person.

Until I discovered the truth.

I was a church-going, active Christian husband and father striving for "balance" between work and home life. Until some finely-tuned suffering became an opportunity for me to learn something profound. There is no hole so deep as the hopeless emptiness of trying to have it all. Through my wife and family, I received a clear vision and purpose, and God orchestrated a stark choice between setting my heart on success in this world or on something better. I gave up my lukewarm, comfortable life and God saw fit to rescue me from that path, and now He won't let me go.

Over the past several years I've had countless conversations with friends about my choice, friends deeply struggling to excel in their fields and in God's Kingdom. This little memo was born out of my desire to show them what the journey out of that trap looked like for me.

ONE
TROPHIES

I had great parents. My dad was a Spanish teacher and a coach, who painted houses in the summer when school was out. He was a loving, present father who disciplined the right way and showed affection to his kids. My mother stayed at home until we were in school and then she worked *in* our school to be close to us. They weren't perfect, but they were good and loving.

But I honestly don't remember them telling me to do my homework. I'm sure they did. I know they read with me as a kid. But I don't remember them ever commanding me in that parental tone to do my homework. For some reason, I always wanted to do well in school, get good grades, please my parents and teachers, and all that nauseating stuff. As I look back I can see now it was a big competition for me, and it began early on, very early on. I can't tell you exactly when, but it must have been before first grade.

I remember when my little classmates and I were being taught the importance of reading. This was before the dawn of the "self-esteem" movement so each of us had to read in front of the class even if it meant peeing yourself from pure terror (which, in fact, Lenny in the chair next to me did). Most kids experienced trauma over having to demonstrate their shaky beginner-level reading skills. Not me. I remember waiting with unbridled anticipation to be called on so that I could show my teachers and my peers how well I could lift the words from the page and speak them into their adoring and envious ears. Positive recognition from a teacher for reading "See Spot Run" well in front of the class gave me a rush and I wanted more.

What is it that drove me? I don't know. Maybe my denigrating nickname at the time caused me to want to compensate. Back then a popular doll that girls played with was "Strawberry Shortcake." I was at least a head-length shorter than all the other kids, including the girls, for most of my childhood. So my nickname became "Shortcake Drake", or "Shortcake" for short. Maybe my drive to be the smartest, fastest, scrappiest, coolest, most talented, teacher-loved, and girl attracting kid was because I had to literally look up at other kids all the time.

From an early age I wanted to do be looked up to by the other kids. I wanted my teachers to say nice things about me. I wanted my parents to be proud of me. I wanted girls to like me. And I realized all of that happened when I did well at something. And my little brain grasped even then the simple concept that the more you achieve, the more people like you, and do and say nice things to you. My desire for success, to be at the top, was deep down in my DNA and it manifested itself in everything, from the classroom to the kickball field.

As I said, my father was a coach, and particularly a track and cross-country coach. So my brother and I naturally were runners. Although we were both good runners, my brother, Dieter, was the most successful runner of the two of us, and he dedicated himself to the sport. I hedged my bets by also playing soccer and wrestling. But no matter what sport we played, the focal point of our existence in my brother's and my life every year between 5th and 8th grade was our middle school's annual distance race around the school grounds.

My brother would wake me up at 5:00 in the morning before school so we could go for a run to train for the race. Mind you this was upstate New York, always a very cold place at 5:00 in the morning except for about 3 days in August. This race was a big deal to us. My brother always won, and I always got second. The competition factor was big for us. We wanted to win. There were huge (for that age) crowds of cheering kids, teachers, and parents at the finish line. And I noticed from even then that the crowd was the loudest and most excited for the winners, and like a dying party horn, the crowd got quieter and quieter until the depressing sound of the last runner's feet pounding the grass was louder than the clapping.

I wanted the cheering to be for me. I wanted my father and my big brother to think highly of me and tell me how good I was.

My brother was the best runner our school had ever seen, and we had some very good runners throughout the school's history. My father built the running program in our school district from the ground up and over 35 years it became one of the most prominent programs in New York State, a state that is known as a powerhouse for running. Dieter began breaking records and was the best runner on the team even as a freshman, superseding the upperclassmen. I looked up and saw the accolades he received and it drove me to want to make a name for myself. I knew I couldn't match his running abilities, so, as I said, I hedged my bets and focused on wrestling in the winter season.

When I was in 8th grade, I weighed a colossal 95 pounds, but that gave me the ability to earn a spot on the Varsity wrestling team at the 98-pound weight class. That meant I could wear a Varsity letter jacket in middle school—something no one else had accomplished in my 8th grade class. My brother had earned it, but very few others. I had the wool jacket with the leather arms and the sewn-on varsity letter, but that wasn't enough for me. In New York State, if you were a state qualifier, you were given a big patch that you would sew onto your varsity letter jacket. The top three wrestlers in that weight class earned a regional patch. I remember the absolute goal for me was to have a patch on my jacket that year. And I clawed my way to the match for a chance to win it, wrestling an upperclassman. And I won. That patch meant more to me than anything else at the time. It was the crown jewel of my existence.

When I got to high school, nothing changed, but the training was tougher and the competition was intense. My brother still had to wake me up at 5:00 in the morning to run before school. It went something like this:

"Get up."

(Snore)

"Get up, slacker."

Then I would hear the door shut behind him. I didn't want to be a disappointment so I'd throw on my spandex for a 3-mile "light" run in the chilly dark. After school it was 5 or 6 miles, and speed drills toward the end of the season. Serious stuff for teenagers. My brother was a star and I had to catch up.

We did well and won a lot. I wore my letter jacket as much as possible so everyone would know what I had accomplished. That feeling of walking through the school halls in that jacket with all the "I am great" patches all over it was intoxicating for a while. I played soccer with the same group of guys for 8 years, and we were good. But I wasn't on the top-tier of the team, just solidly in the middle. So, being excessively pragmatic, I gave up soccer and my long-lasting friendships with those guys to focus on what I was best at—running. When I saw the soccer crew, I made sure I had my patch-laden varsity jacket on to prove I had accomplished more. Which meant I was better than them. But soon I realized that no one seemed to care much. It wasn't bringing me the expected daily congratulations and adoration—the only currency of childhood success—and it began to sink in that it wasn't glorious at all if no one thought it so. A wool jacket and a bunch of trophies wasn't enough.

Then, in the middle of that high school self-analyzing, ego-shattering experience something strange happened. My Uncle Jack happened. Uncle Jack is my father's cousin. My father and his sisters, my aunts, had always spoken of Uncle Jack, and he took on a mythical image in my mind. I learned through family lore that this is a man who achieved at the top levels of everything he tried, becoming the valedictorian of his high school class, top honors in college, and in his graduate work in seminary, then landing a coveted pastor position at the largest church of his denomination in the area. He was pushed by his parents to be the best, and he was. He was the shining star.

But when I met Uncle Jack he wasn't a shining star at all. He was dirty and had holes in his shoes. He was homeless. Somehow he found his way walking to our house and he showed up one day out of the blue. My parents, not knowing what else to do, welcomed him into our home. I'd known about "poor Uncle Jack" who "lost it," had thrown his pastor garb in the dumpster behind his church one day and taken off. He had carried a heavy burden of striving to live up to his mother's high standards of excellence into adulthood and one day it simply became too much. Maybe it'd been coming a long time, or maybe it was a spurious decision. I only knew him through stories, how he went to live on an Indian reservation to better understand the plight of Native Americans, how he went to Brooklyn in the late 60's during the race riots. And now here was Uncle Jack, penniless and homeless. Everyone seemed to feel sorry for him, except Uncle Jack.

I was extremely curious at the time, and fascinated by this man who was brilliant and accomplished in an earlier life, but now homeless. He did suffer from mental illness and I don't know if he was on or off of his medication at the time. My parents saw how fascinated I was by Uncle Jack and pulled me aside to explain that he didn't have full control of his mental faculties. I got it, I completely understood the "danger" of Uncle Jack on my impressionable life, but it made no difference to me. He spoke of God, Jesus, the "Lord", praying, the Bible, and he believed in these things that we couldn't see with our eyes. I saw a man who had something I didn't have—faith. And although his thoughts were random and scattering, and his life on the surface was a complete shambles, he had in his heart something that I was just beginning to understand eluded me—peace and joy.

Uncle Jack traveled from one men's shelter or rescue mission to the next, crossing the country on foot mostly, but sometimes with the help of a generous trucker willing to give him a ride. He went from Massachusetts to South Dakota, Georgia to Michigan. I asked him how he found food every day since he didn't have any income, and he told me how he had some money saved from an inheritance, but often he didn't have access to it when all banks were local and his bank was in another state, and so he would be walking along the road hungry but believing that His Father in heaven would give him just what he needed when he needed it, because, very simply, that is what God promises in the Bible. And not long after he would find a bag of food discarded on the side of the road where he was walking.

Uncle Jack stayed with us only for a couple of days, but while we were together he told me story after story like this, and I could tell that this wasn't some fabricated hallucination, but he really did believe that God provided for him, and God really showed up day after day in what we would call miraculous ways. But for him it was just a way of life.

I remember feeling that this man wasn't so different, just a little off socially perhaps. It was the rest of us that were off the mark. He had something I wanted, but it was just a feeling at the time. I don't know what intrigued me so much about him. He just did. How could anyone possibly be at peace and have joy who didn't know where their next meal would come from and who had no place to call home? How could this man who was brilliant and successful leave it all behind?

As time went on I settled my questions with the only *logical* answer: He must not be right in the head. Uncle Jack was marginalized in our family for leaving the way he did, mental illness or not, and his religiosity didn't bode well. He was radical, and highly intriguing, but no one wanted to talk about him. And despite my fascination, I didn't tell any of my friends about him. Religious kids weren't cool, and I didn't want to be un-cool, even though I projected an image of independence and self-sufficiency. So I moved on, but I never forgot Uncle Jack.

High school was coming to a close and the obvious next step was college. Because my father was a teacher in my high school I knew all the teachers, guidance counselors, and administrators, and they knew me. There's a special place that teachers have in their hearts for other teachers' kids who do well in school, and I always felt the encouragement of my teachers. They, like my parents, wanted me to do well in a particular way. So when it came time to go off to college there were high hopes.

I applied to a total of 2 schools. I wasn't exactly hedging my bets. One school was Cornell, an Ivy League school in Central New York State, and the other was a relatively unknown school in Virginia that hardly anyone ever heard of except that it was named for a dead president, James Madison. I got into both. And it came time to decide between the two. There I was, sitting at my desk in my bedroom staring at the acceptance letters of each school wondering what the heck to do. The cost never really was an issue because it was fairly equivalent between the two. My mind went back to the campus tours my parent's and I took.

I remember walking through Cornell's campus. Someone made a comment about a target being painted on the rock bed at the bottom of the ravine underneath one of the bridges spanning the many rock cliffs throughout the grounds. It turns out the suicide rate is pretty high at Cornell and someone thought that would be a great joke. I thought it was pretty funny at the time. And all I could remember about JMU was that the girls were almost all blondes.

Suicide or blondes? Suicide or blondes? Hmm . . . .

The blondes won me over.

My parents were pretty happy for me, for whatever reason. As I look back now, maybe they were just happy because JMU was 3 states away so I wouldn't be home every weekend. But I remember talking to my teachers, who invested their time and effort in me and rightfully had a stake in my success. Somehow, they all knew I got into Cornell. I'm sure I let just the right people know so that they would tell everyone else so that I could keep up the appearance of humility. When the inevitable question came up, "So, where did you decide to go to college?" and I told them, first the question was, "Where is that?" and then that subtle smile of disappointment would appear at the corner of their mouth. I had the opportunity to be one of the school's academic trophies on the wall and represent at an Ivy League school, but I was passing that up.

What was worse than the response of my teachers, who at least had the maturity to wish me well, was that of my friends. My "smart" friends, who along side me had spent their lives slaving over AP text books, giving their all to achieve academic success so that they would be rewarded with acceptance letters to Harvard, Yale, Columbia, and Cornell couldn't begin to understand my decision. Even my jock friends who looked up to me for my athletic prowess knew that forsaking an Ivy League school was nuts. Kids don't yet have social graces at 17 years old, and I could feel their ridicule. I had definitely fallen from grace in their eyes and that was brutal.

After experiencing their subtle mockery I felt a sting inside because a part of me agreed with them. It made no sense really why after chasing success my entire young life I chose a school that seemed, well, so . . . mediocre in comparison. At the time I didn't understand it myself. And it would take another 15 years for me to figure out why I made that decision.

TWO
COINCIDENCE

Early experiences shape our personalities in ways none of us ever fully understands. When I was about 8 years old, my parents invited some family friends to live with us while their new house was being built. I guess they needed a place to stay in the interim so our house became their house for a few months. It was my Spanish teacher dad taking the "mi casa, tu casa" thing seriously. We always had friends over at our house, especially in the summer, so I remember it feeling very normal.

The oldest boy was delegated to my and my brother's room, so for a time there were three of us in the windowless basement bedroom. One night I woke with my bladder ready to explode. So I sprang out of bed only to realize I didn't know where I was in the pitch-blackness. We normally had a night-light, but probably because of the big kid in our room it was turned off. I tiptoed around that room, arms stretched out, for who knows how long feeling for anything familiar. I eventually made it to a wall, but then I wasn't sure which wall it was. I couldn't find the light switch or a door handle. I just knew I was going to fill my spider man footie-pajamas right there in front of my brother and the older kid, start crying, and die of embarrassment. I'm not exactly sure why, but that traumatized me like nothing else I'd lived through to that point.

When I was in high school, that same feeling came back to me from time to time. High school for me began well with a lot of fun, a lot of friends, and a relationship with a girl I liked a lot. But it got progressively more depressing for me. I was becoming more aware of myself and the world around me, more in tune with the pulse of life, or lack thereof. The focus of my life up to that point was achievement—in academics, in sports, in social status, attracting girls, etc. But none of the trophies, patches, class rankings, or girlfriends brought me what Uncle Jack had: peace, and joy. And they certainly didn't bring me what I wanted most: love. I got short-lived attention, maybe a reference in a local newspaper after winning a race or a wrestling match, but not love.

At times, when I was alone, that feeling of terror, wandering in the pitch-black darkness and finding no way out came over me. Except now I felt my wandering would end up taking me over a cliff to a bottomless pit. This was my conviction in my heart. All of my accomplishments in sports, in school, and in popularity meant absolutely nothing, and I knew it. I was blind and in the process of my wandering I had done wrong at every turn.

We didn't read the Bible in our family, and we didn't talk about God. I'm sure my parents believed in God, but we just didn't talk about religious things. So I didn't have an explanation for my feelings, my fear of that blindness, and the deep sense that for all my achievements, I was still blind with no idea how to find my way through life. I knew I had broken some of my parent's rules, but my guilt for choosing the wrong things was deeper than being disobedient. Contemplating my mortality, I knew that there must be a God and He could not be happy with the life I had chosen. I don't know how, but I knew who I was, and that I wasn't whom He'd made me to be. When I thought about my death, there was no night-light to guide me. All I saw was darkness, and all I felt was the certainty of free falling off that cliff in utter darkness and plunging into the pit.

The thoughts and feelings I had about God were vague and general in high school, heavy on the feeling and light on the thought. They were real feelings of fear and confusion, but I didn't know exactly where they came from or how they got there. In the last 2 years of high school any deep thought I had, including those about God, were marked with sadness.

I thought at the time that a lot of my depression was because of my circumstances. I had a girlfriend my sophomore and junior years whom I found messing around with a friend of mine. That pretty much killed any notion of being able to trust people.

I didn't have any friends that I could really relate to, or who I felt really cared anything about me. And painting the walls of my bedroom black with Pink Floyd's *Dark Side of the Moon* album cover art was a bad choice when I least needed my physical surroundings to enforce the darkness in my spirit. There was deep sadness and darkness in me and I didn't think anyone except my mother wanted to hear anything about it. My mother was wonderful to me, as she was the only one who could draw me out and listen to find the core of my problems. But when I was a teenager I wanted someone else to listen to me and care. I so desperately wanted someone to validate what I was feeling and love me out of the problems in my head that I couldn't shake on my own.

When I was getting ready to ship off to college, I was sure that everything would change. I would be in college, around new people who didn't know that I was a head-case, and I could start over. My mother and sister drove me down to JMU, helped me unpack in my new freshman dorm, then my mom cried outside with all the other moms who were leaving their "innocent lambs" to the "wolves" of college life.

A bunch of upperclassmen came back to school a couple of days early to volunteer to help the freshmen carry their stuff from their parents' cars to the dorms. A couple of those guys were there at the curb waiting for me to open the door so they could help me carry my trash bags full of clothes up to my all-male dorm. I thought it was great of them to do all this, but I didn't really understand their motivation. It made very little sense to me.

When they were done helping me haul my stuff, they told me they were part of InterVarsity Christian Fellowship which was hosting a big gathering for the freshmen that night, and there would be watermelon. My new roommate, Kevin, and I mulled it over, but it didn't sound very cool. Keg party yes, Christian watermelon bash no.

We decided to go after the realization that it was our best shot at meeting some girls. Trotting across the railroad tracks that ran through campus, we made it to the field where almost all the new freshmen were standing around spitting out seeds in as cool a fashion as possible. Kevin and I avoided the watermelon and found our new, across-the-bathroom, ROTC buddy Neal, who told us we needed to follow him. He strolled us over to a row of blondes that he had been talking to. The very first girl I met was Jaye, and she was blonde.

I remember that night so clearly. I can't tell you exactly what words were exchanged because there were so many people around. But I remember sensing that Jaye was different than any girl I had known before. She asked me questions about myself and took a sincere interest in hearing about me. Not in a romantic sense, but just as one human being caring for another, even though we had just met and we were in the middle of a crowd of people. And that sense became more clear when I found out later that night as a group of us continued to hang out that she had a boyfriend of several years. Then I knew she wasn't just "checking me out" (but I was definitely checking her out).

Kevin and I, along with a group of Jaye's friends, ended up in her dorm room and the first thing I noticed was a sticker on her wall that said, "With God there are no coincidences." I stared at that sticker for a while. I had no idea then how important that phrase would be in my life and how believing it would underpin so much that would happen to me.

That same week, the first week of school, I passed a couple of old men in suits handing out little green Bibles. I never had a Bible before, and I was curious, so I gladly took one and tucked it away quickly in my pocket. I read that thing in secret like there was no tomorrow, but didn't have the foggiest idea what it was saying, not being an adequate student of 17th century English. But for possibly the first time in my life, I wasn't motivated by the desire for attention or to impress anyone whatsoever. I simply wanted answers.

A couple of weeks later I was between classes so I dropped in the dining hall to grab lunch. I was sitting alone reading the JMU newspaper when an upperclassman came up to me with his tray of d-hall food and asked if he could sit with me. "Sure" I said, thinking it was weird, but whatever.

This guy was just like Jaye, only male and with a beard. He showed the same authentic interest in me as a person. You know, a person who asks real questions about you and doesn't look like it's an obligation? His name was Jason. A friend of his came up to him and they chatted about the Bible study they were doing together. I don't know what got into me, but I interrupted them and asked what they were talking about. My sense of coolness usually prevented me from entering into the religious realm. Jason and I chatted a little longer and he told me about a friend of his who could talk to me a little more about it if I wanted. How did he know I wanted?

So he took down my name and number. Random.

It must have been over a month later that I got a knock on my dorm room door and a big 6'3" guy about 45 years old shows up telling me that his friend Jason met me in d-hall and gave him my dorm room address. He said he was getting together with a couple of other college guys to read the Bible to find out what it says, and he asked if I wanted to join them. "Definitely" I said, wanting to make sense of the thees, thous and wouldsts, etc. "My name is Steve," he said.

I didn't have any hesitation about doing it. No one there knew, but I was desperate to find an answer for the fear I felt, and the deep psychological pain it caused me, pain that wasn't inflicted on me by anyone or any specific circumstance. Why did I feel I was in mortal trouble? Where did this profound sense of *wrongness* come from? I wasn't one of those "bad" kids; I was a good kid, at least on the surface and in the daylight. So why did I feel this way? It made no sense, but I knew that if there was another dimension to me that I hadn't understood, then I wanted to shed light on it so that I could know what it was. The little I could make sense of in my little green Bible seemed to hold some clues as to what that was all about, so the study group was a welcome invitation. He said that we would probably start up after Christmas break.

Jaye and I became really good friends during that time. I was truly amazed by her joy and gentle, consistent, and authentic love for people, and her complete lack of insecurity. I was interested in her, but the 6'4" baseball boyfriend was a major obstacle given my "Shortcake Drake" complex, so I didn't pursue it much. We were just friends.

Then, in one of my drunken bus rides with my buddies to an off-campus party, we sat behind a couple of guys from another college. I yelled up to them sitting in the front of the bus.

"Where are you guys from?" I shouted with a toothy grin.

The dude with a big wad of dip in his lip said, "Fairfax."

"No kidding. What high school did you go to?"

"Fairfax High," he said.

"Fairfax? Do you know Jaye and Carrie?" I asked Mr. Dip. "Jaye and Carrie" were roommates now at JMU and as inseparable as always.

Big Dipper stood up and said that he was one of their best friends, and then he stumbled to hang out with us in the back of the bus to continue the slurred conversation.

"I've known Jaye and Carrie since we were little," he told me. "I'm best friends with Jaye's boyfriend." Even in my inebriation I could smell an opportunity.

"Really? So you're good friends?" I asked.

"Best friends. We played ball together."

"No kidding. So . . . he and Jaye are pretty tight, huh?" I thought I would snoop a little and get the inside edge.

He leaned over to me with his bulging bottom lip and quasi-whispered, "Nah, they're on the outs. I think he's seeing other people."

No kidding! Now I had the scoop I needed to know that there was an opening. After that Jaye and I grew closer as she and baseball-boy grew apart.

Jaye and Carrie got involved in InterVarsity Christian Fellowship that first semester. They called it "I.V." for short. She went to all their meetings and did Bible studies with other girls. That was good for her, I thought. When I knew she had a meeting that night, I would make fun of her, asking if she was going to the HIV meeting. Sure, I made fun of her, but I would discretely find out where they were meeting, and a couple of times I snuck in the back door and peeked in to find out what it was all about. I heard music and clapping, but didn't stick around long for fear of being caught. I wasn't looking for Jaye, necessarily. I was peeking in to find out about this religious stuff.

When we got back to JMU after Christmas break, Steve called me up and said he was ready to start the little study to investigate what the Bible was all about. We started looking at the book of John. There were two other guys in the group, but I was the only one that seemed like he wanted to be there. Man, I was into it. I saw with my own eyes, not through a preacher, that the Bible, and Jesus himself, claimed Jesus was God. And that it claims he did miracles to prove he wasn't some yahoo. And how he healed people and loved them. And then John 3:16. Whoever believes in him will not be destroyed but will live forever. I thought of the pit I was sure I would fall into.

About 4 weeks into it, none of the other guys showed up. Steve and I waited, but they must have had better things to do. Steve told me to wait there, that he had to find something. He must have been gone for 10 minutes looking when he opened the door and walked in with nothing more than a napkin in his hand. I started to wonder if Steve wasn't a little strange at that moment.

He asked if he could share something with me, and I told him of course he could. So he began to draw what started out looking like a *Far Side* cartoon but morphed into a depiction of 2 sides of a giant canyon, and he began writing down certain passages of the Bible around the illustration. He turned to those passages and asked me to read them. God was on one side of the canyon, and man on the other. I saw how God had created me, and that God is eternal, without end.

I read about how we had all fallen because of the things we think, say, and do, and no matter what we try to do there is nothing that will bridge the gap between us and God. In the end, we'll all face death and then we'll face God to account for all of our life. And that separation is real and forever. It's darkness. Everything I saw on that napkin shouted at me. A light came on and exposed a giant jigsaw puzzle that finally came together in my heart and mind. Everything fit, and I could see across that pit for the first time.

The other side was all still a little vague to me, but I saw light nonetheless, and having wandered blindly for years I now suddenly saw that there was something else out there. In that light, I could see that my sense of wrongness was a *spiritual* understanding that came from choosing the life I had. I had broken the law of God. The path I was on would lead to the dark pit where I would have to pay for breaking that law. I saw that my pain was remorse over my sin and my sadness in having no way out of its penalty.

Then Steve drew a big cross between the two sides of the canyon. He didn't need to open up the Bible to the other passages—I knew. Jesus was the bridge across and the only way to cross over from the darkness that I was in into the forever light of God was through Jesus. I got it. And I believed it. The only Christian song I knew was Amazing Grace and that day it became real for me. My eyes were opened and I could see. Not long after that was the first time that I slept, really slept, in a very long time. I look back and realize that I knew almost nothing of the life God wanted for me. I had broken his law and now I was forgiven because Jesus paid it all for me.

After my life-changing meeting with Steve, I sprang back to my dorm room and found Jaye there conspiring with my roommates to make a candlelit dinner for me. Coincidental? Jaye was the first person I told about my new faith. She didn't believe me. I know it must have seemed like a really bad attempt at getting her to like me more. But over time she began to see little signs of life pop out of me like little pieces of fruit that spring from a once dead branch.

I also became good friends with that upperclassman Jason, who I met in d-hall. He continued to call me up all the time to check up on me and ask if I wanted to meet for lunch between classes. I soaked up all I could from this joyful, peaceful guy. Three years after we met he was graduating and going off to the Middle East to be a missionary. We were standing outside his dorm room and he began telling me that the day we met he was walking up to d-hall, and he did something he didn't normally do. He told me that he stopped halfway up the stairs, paused, and prayed, "God, use me today to help someone to see you." And then he saw me sitting there alone and we met. And he told me that after Steve began reading the Bible with us that a whole group began praying for God to help us guys see Him, to know Him, and to know His peace.

Meeting Jaye and seeing in her what I now know is true love, joy, peace, patience, kindness, gentleness, faithfulness, goodness, and self-control, and then meeting Jason and Steve and seeing it in them was no coincidence. I didn't plan it, and they didn't plan it either. But God planned it. They were in love with God because they knew God loved them, and all that good stuff just came out of them, and I was attracted to it like moth to a flame. God used them to draw me into His kingdom and I have eternity to thank them for it.

When I first crossed over into the Kingdom of God, it was like crossing over the Grand Canyon. Although I was in God's family, I felt like I was still right there on the edge at times, not worrying about falling, but still able to look back and clearly see what it was I came from. And I was still close enough to the other side that I could still see my friends who hadn't crossed over and who were still blind like I was.

Not long after I started following Jesus, I got a wild hair to join a fraternity. I have no idea why. It's not as if I set out to save the brothers. I think I just liked the idea of being in a club. It wasn't a good idea, given my lack of discipline at beer parties. Getting hammered still seemed like an okay thing to do. I know Jesus turned water into wine at a party, and was thrown nasty slurs for hanging out with "sinners" like the type of guys and girls that go to fraternity parties every Friday and Saturday night (and occasional Monday through Thursday). But I don't think he did the stuff I did. I don't think he did flaming tequila shots while dancing to Pearl Jam to impress the disciples. I'm glad he spent time with people at those types of parties, but I'm glad he didn't do what I did. I was a Christian, a forgiven man, once and for all, but I still wanted to be cool. I still wanted to belong and impress people.

I grew close to a group of guys in my pledge class. The recipe for catalyzing fraternal brotherhood one chilly October weekend was $3 wine and an all-night campfire in the middle of the Virginia woods with no sleeping bags. But beyond the usual bonding that happens to a pledge class who have to bond together to endure weekly cleaning up of who-knows-what off the walls, floor and ceiling, there was a core group of guys I clicked with and over that semester my heart was broken for them.

I never cared much about other people before; I only cared about how they treated me. But I started to care about these guys. I looked back from the edge across the chasm that Jesus brought me across and saw them. They were cool and tough, but a few hours into the parties, deep into chemical bliss, a few of them lost their inhibitions and were open to talking about God and their lack of direction.

My friend and fellow pledge, Brian, came from a big Irish Catholic family, and half of his siblings became Christians. Brian liked to smoke green leafy stuff at parties and then he was wide open to talking to me about Jesus. Without it he was much like most people, guarded. He knew some of the right answers to the religious questions, but just wasn't willing to put his life in Jesus' hands and cross over. He struggled a lot and we spent countless parties talking in a corner about faith and obedience. Brian always had sadness in his eyes. You can always tell those who have been beaten up by the world; they have a defeated, despondent look. Others are ambitious and their eyes look hungry for the kill. Brian's sad eyes told me his anesthesia wasn't working against his deeper pain.

Halfway through my semester of pledging I knew my purpose there. I had experienced enough conversations about Jesus with different guys in the fraternity that I started to see that maybe God had a purpose for me there. I meant it for fun and belonging, but God had other plans, and I started to get the picture. A bunch of the guys didn't like my faith, especially when I got convicted in my heart about drinking and gave it up. But most respected it. I didn't really care either way; it was guys like my fellow pledges Brian, Hugh, Ian, Jimmy, and Jason that kept me there.

I was so bold with them, challenging them to read the Bible and consider Jesus. I was raw, they were raw, but they were the best conversations about God with people who don't believe that I've ever had. Even though Steve was spending time with me reading and studying the Bible and I was learning, there had to be a ton of pseudo-theological garbage coming out of my mouth, but my heart was committed to those guys, or at least I thought.

• • •

My roommate, Mike, decided to pledge the fraternity the next semester, after seeing the fun I was having. But halfway into his pledge period, some of the brothers got together and decided to blackball Mike, a not-so-cool way to kick someone out before they become an official member. It made no sense to me at the time, but later I thought that maybe it was because they didn't want another Bible-thumper.

I was already a brother and they couldn't get rid of me, but they still had veto power over Mike. It's not as if I turned into Oliver Cromwell, forcing Puritanism on the unwilling fraternity. I just stopped drinking and started reading the Bible with a few of the guys. And the ironic thing was that Mike wasn't even a Christian. He was only guilty by room mating. That whole episode really ticked me off, and it hurt, so I retreated from the fraternity. They kept me on because I helped them keep their charter with my GPA, but that was about it. It was an indirect rejection of me, and I reciprocated with passive-aggressive rejection of them.

I spent more time with my new Christian friends and with Jaye. And as I grew in my new life and faith, over time, I noticed that I knew fewer and fewer people who didn't know Jesus. Most of the people I spent time with were Christians, who were good influences on my life, but I felt that I had less and less in common with people who were still on the other side of the canyon. It became just easier to spend time with people who shared my values and who spoke the same language. As I "grew" in my faith, I moved farther and farther away from the edge of the canyon where I could see my friends on the other side who are still walking around blind. Their voices became distant and muted and my vision of them became blurry. Soon, I'd all but forgotten about helping the blind see.

My green-leaf friend Brian tracked me down the first week after summer break of our senior year at JMU. We had lost touch over the past 2 years, but he found me on campus. He was a different guy, excited and smiling a lot. He began to tell me how he accepted Jesus over the summer with his brother helping him. He had such joy and peace; it was truly an incredible difference. His eyes had light pouring out of them. And my heart swelled with joy for my friend who could see now.

I knew seeing a friend come into real life, the *only real* life, was more important and significant than any GPA or award. But I wanted Steve and my Christian friends to know about Brian. Not only for his sake or theirs, but for mine. I wanted the validation, to show some sort of accomplishment, like a Boy Scout badge, as if I had anything to do with the God of the universe intervening in Brian's life and rescuing him from the pit. Nonetheless I wanted people to know because it still seemed like a trophy and I knew I would win godliness points with it. I seemed "successful" again, only now in a Christian sort of way.

I look back at that time now and realize a lot about myself. The mere fact that 12,000 people my age surrounded me in college meant easy opportunities for fast relationships with so many different kinds of people. It was so easy to call up a buddy, or run into a friend, and talk for hours without serious pressures. Conversations were easy to find because no one was really that worried about their classes, at least not worried enough to miss out on deep mutual contemplation of our lives and the universe. And it was easy to sprinkle the conversations with Jesus to my wandering and blind friends. In that sense, I wish life could stay like college forever.

But it doesn't.

THREE
SANTA

It didn't take long after I started reading the bible to see that God is love, and I experienced His love when I realized that I was forgiven, once and for all time, and that one day I will meet him face to face and He will welcome me in because He chose to forgive me in 1992. The questions began to arise in my heart about what it means for God to love me in my daily life. What does that look like? I wondered if His love meant that He would solve all my problems and give me good gifts. I wondered if He really does pay attention to the details of my life.

Growing up in my house, you would have thought Santa Claus was a part of the family in December. We wrote letters to him every year, we left him cookies and milk that he always ate, we put the fire out Christmas eve so he wouldn't get burned on the way down the 8" diameter chimney flu, and he would leave us a bunch of presents under the tree in return. There wasn't any doubt in my mind that he was real—I could see the evidence of him on Christmas morning. And besides, everyone said he was real. There were countless songs and movies about him, so why would I doubt? I didn't doubt.

When I found out, I was more than bummed. But after I analyzed the lifelong deception, I came to the conclusion that it didn't really matter. After all, what I cared mostly about were the gifts I received and whether it said "From Santa" or "From Mommy and Daddy" made absolutely no difference in the final analysis. Being fooled wasn't a good feeling, but then being treated like one of the "big kids" who were on the side of the truth compensated for it. I could still perpetuate the legend to my little sister, which was cool because I knew the truth and she didn't.

When I first believed in Jesus and all He is, and started calling God my Father, I really did believe. But there were times I wondered deep down in the places of my heart I didn't want to tell anyone about if it was all maybe just a little like Santa. I believed, but I wanted to see evidence of Him not just in the Bible or in books, but in my life. And I was too much of a realist and a cynic to claim anything to be of God that wasn't really supernatural. I didn't want any wishful thinking to turn into a testimony that I told everyone about only to find out when I get to Heaven that I was wrong.

Dating Jaye in college, one would think that my depression and insecurities would evaporate. Here I had this beautiful girlfriend who was the most loving, peaceful person I had ever met, who never gave me any reason whatsoever to not trust her, and instead of eliminating my head problems, they got worse. I think it might have been because I knew I had a treasure in her, beyond any other girl I had dated, and the fear of losing her amplified my insecurities.

Here was the test. Would I fall into my usual pattern of questioning her sincerity and kindness to me, or accept it and trust? Would I look for affirmation and devotion to me in every phone call and every phrase, or be patient and let the relationship develop?

It wasn't a decision, actually, but it was a test, and I failed. I wish I could have had the power to decide, but I didn't. Jaye had a lot of friends from high school at JMU, and had made a lot of new friends at InterVarsity and her dorm, who naturally wanted to get to know her, and she them. One time there was a mixed group of people from IV who asked Jaye and Carrie to go out with them on a Friday night. It was an innocent gathering of friends, but to me it was a decision on Jaye's part to *not* spend time with me. I sat in the dark for hours that night in my bed, steaming with sadness and hurt. And about the time I thought Jaye would be coming home, I got up out of bed and crossed the railroad tracks that divided the campus and which separated my dorm from hers. There was a line of trees in front of the field outside her dorm entrance, where she would return from the night out. I sat there, waiting to see her, if she was with another guy, to see if she *really* was devoted to me. There was absolutely nothing in her character to make me question logically, but that made no difference. I couldn't see past my fears and distrust.

Towards the end of our first year at JMU, I really put Jaye through it. I constantly questioned her talking to guys and wondered out loud about her feelings for me. I put her through agony week after week because of my whacked-out behavior. Jaye saw something in me to hang on the way she did, even though her best friend and roommate Carrie hated my guts, and rightly so for the jerk that I was. My bouts of depression in my dorm room were rough, and when I saw Jaye the next day I looked to her to solve my problems, but she couldn't. I met with Big Steve to tell me the verses from the Bible that I could read to solve my problems. We read the verses, but it didn't help. We prayed, but it didn't work.

In the months leading up to the end of our freshman year, I decided to take a job in the Northern Virginia area for the summer so I could be near Jaye, whose parents lived in Fairfax. It was a house painting business that I would run. A dorm buddy had some family friends that said they would rent a room out to me. I found an old beat up blue painting van that I bought to haul paint and ladders. I wouldn't be with my family, but I would be near Jaye. I was set for a great summer.

School ended, and Jaye and I loaded up our stuff in my van to drive to Northern Virginia. She said she needed to talk to me, and 2 hours alone in the blue monster would be a good enough setting. We drove onto the highway, and over the smell of burnt oil and old paint she said that we needed a break from each other. All the irrational fear and insecurity that I brought to the relationship needed to be dealt with, and she realized that my problems couldn't be solved while we were together. In retrospect, it really was amazing wisdom, but at the time it pretty much blew my world apart. I didn't blame her for it. Somehow, I knew she was right.

So I dropped her off at her parent's house, and dreadfully dragged myself away to live with this family I didn't know, in a city I was completely unfamiliar with, to work a business that I was totally unprepared for. I knew all of this going into it, but it was based on the premise that I would be able to spend the summer with Jaye. Now that the purpose was gone, the bleak details of daily life that I glossed over began to rear their ugly head. I was alone. Incredibly alone.

My pain was intense during that time. I prayed every night in tears for God to take away my fears and insecurities. Jaye had given me an Amy Grant tape, which was the only music I owned that spoke of God. I wore out that cassette, using it to help me get through the heartache. I was miserable, and I couldn't find a way out. I wanted to change, but no matter what I did the fear and insecurity only grew more and more intense, which was now coupled with deep sadness.

Jaye and her family were going to visit family in Germany for two weeks, and Jaye's dad, knowing I was now a house painter, asked me to move into their house while they were gone so I could paint a bunch of rooms and surprise Jaye's mom when they got back. And I could also help take care of Chico, their mangy little dog who once looked like Benji but now looked like the canine version of Chucky because of his bout with doggy psoriasis. I agreed to do it to help them out, but I knew it would be horrible for me staying in Jaye's room for two weeks, being reminded daily of the girl I loved but who was being ripped away from me by my own deep problems.

Night after night I spent in Jaye's bedroom praying for God to take away my fears, to change me. I was completely and totally alone in their house, and so my voice could carry throughout the house and I wouldn't be heard by anyone. My prayer was uninhibited by any potential embarrassment because I had no audience but God.

One night, about halfway through the two weeks, there I was again praying in Jaye's room. It was dark, but there was just enough light to make out the pictures on the walls. This time I was literally on my knees in the middle of her room, and I was desperate. I prayed and prayed, asking God to take this away from me. And tears poured down my cheeks, knowing I had been here many times before, praying the same prayer, feeling the same pain, but I couldn't change.

I opened my eyes, and saw a plaque on a stand on Jaye's dresser. It was a wooden painted plaque with printed words. It said simply on top, "Love." And underneath it said, "Love is patient, love is kind, it does not envy, it does not boast, it is not proud. Love is not rude or selfish or easily angered, it keeps no record of wrongs. Love does not delight in evil but rejoices in the truth. It always protects, always trusts, always hopes, always perseveres. Love never fails." I read it for the first time that night, even though I had read it before. The truth of those words sunk deep in my heart and I could literally feel it warming me inside.

Ever since meeting Uncle Jack and observing his unexplainable peace and joy I longed for what he had. I found that when I put my faith in Jesus. I found the truth, which told me that I was forgiven for every last thing I had done wrong and for the good and right things that I had left undone. I had peace with God. I saw that it was God who initiated in my life because He loves me.

The love I knew of God was real, yes, but it seemed vague, distant, and in many ways intangible. I saw that I was part of His grand plan and that He rescued me, but did He love me specifically in daily ways? I was carried over to the side of life, but was I on my own now to figure this life out? I wasn't sure. The peace I experienced and accepted was real, however my deep longing for love wasn't satisfied.

What I understood at that moment, reading that plaque, is that my definition of love, until that night, was warped, and what I was seeking that I thought was love, was something completely different. It was an imitation of the real thing. It was a sugar-free, saccharin, hollow Easter egg bunny when I longed for Belgian chocolate. When I longed for what I defined as love, I was looking for adoration, affirmation, and affection. I wasn't looking for someone who was patient with me through my failings, kind to me when I was a jerk, selfless, considerate, who loved truth and goodness, trusting, forgiving, and with all of these things, consistent. And so my expectations of Jaye, as a result, were warped, and so were my actions and reactions. But, in that instant, I knew what true love was and I threw the ugly imitation in the garbage where it belongs.

The tears kept pouring down, now only harder and faster. The pain I had was now joy and elation. I felt as though I had been pulled from a dungeon and chains that held me were gone. I knew something happened. I cannot explain it, but I knew that all of my fears and insecurities were gone. Literally gone. It wasn't a rational experience explained by a psychological breakthrough. I saw the truth of what love is, what God's love is, His practical, daily love, for the first time.

I had read that passage in 1 Corinthians many times before, but God opened my eyes and gave me a heart to understand at just the right time. It was supernatural and remarkably not coincidental. I knew that God took away my fears and taught me what real love is. I had absolutely no doubt about it. In opening my eyes to see that I was looking for Jaye to give what I thought was love, and all the while she was showing me real love, God specifically and personally showed me *His* love for me. He intervened to open my eyes and change my heart, which changed my life.

I couldn't wait for Jaye to get back from Germany so I could tell her. I knew she wouldn't believe me, but I couldn't wait to tell her anyway because I knew it was true.

It was just a few minutes after they pulled into the driveway from the airport that I pulled Jaye aside to tell her that God took away my problems, that I was healed. She gave me a supportive, but "Yeah right" kind of look. I told her she would see it's true.

Over the next few weeks she saw the proof of it. It was truly amazing. This was the first time I saw up close and personal in a tangible, almost mystical way, that God was not Santa Claus. I finally knew for sure that He is real and He really does love me, and He really will intervene in my life for good.

The rest of our college years were amazing. Jaye and I grew deeply in love, after God worked out my insecurities and fears, taught me to accept His grace and love, and He taught me what real love is between people, not the romanticized idea I subscribed to before. I got plugged into a great group of Christian guys, and made some life-long friends that I will never lose. Friends like my buddy Chris, who I roomed with the last 2 years, who taught me how to smoke a pipe, a skill I haven't yet quite grasped. And as God changed me, he made me much more joyful and fun, and even Carrie began to like me.

Jaye and I got married right after graduation, and I started working for a major financial institution. Our life together as a married couple had begun. My fear and insecurities in relationships were gone. But as the realities of providing for my wife and myself, and paying bills, stared me in the face, I discovered another issue in my heart. And God would again show himself to be real in my life.

Everyone has a story about his first car. Some kids get cars for their 16th birthday, whether a Porsche or your dad's old station wagon. Your first car is like a first love, you never forget it. Well I never had a first car of my own. I married into it. When Jaye and I got married she was the only one who had a car. It was a 10-year-old red Honda Civic hatchback that her dad bought from her uncle while she was in college. It was a little tomato. I spiced it up a little—I put on fluffy seat covers, and I pasted a cool black pin stripe down the sides. We were young, in love, and we didn't need much, so the tomato car was great.

Our first apartment was in Arlington, VA. Standing outside our apartment door, you could close your eyes and feel like you were in the kitchen of the United Nations building. A distinct curry smell came from the apartment next door, jalapeños down the hall, and some sort of spicy mystery meat sausage cooking upstairs. I think we were the only white people there, and English was definitely the minority language. And we loved it.

My job took me to our company's headquarters for a couple of weeks every month, which happened to be in the same city as one of Jaye's good college friends. So while I traveled there one week, Jaye came with me to spend time with her friend. One Saturday morning we woke up at her friend's house to find our little red Honda Civic's front fender bashed in, probably hit by a not-so-clear-headed twenty something coming home from the bar. Our little tomato, our only car, was damaged goods. I immediately called our insurance company to inquire about how they were going to fix it only to find out about the realities of insurance—it ain't free. That seemingly unimportant deductible option that I picked when I bought the policy was now coming back to haunt me. We simply didn't have the money for the deductible so we couldn't afford to fix it. The good news was that the car still moved and got us from place to place. The bad news was that Virginia is an inspection state, and our inspection was coming up in a couple of months. The headlight was destroyed so the car wouldn't pass inspection and we wouldn't be able to register the car, our *only* car, which meant I wouldn't be able to get to work. This was our first real dilemma.

I worried like crazy about that car and the inspection, but didn't know what to do. We didn't have the money to repair it at a body shop. It was my job to provide, to take care of my responsibilities as a husband and a man, and I had to take care of this car. I can look back and see that it was irrational, and certainly not the end of the world. But nonetheless, my heart wasn't ready to really believe that God would come through, and therefore it was up to me to make it happen. But I didn't know how. Failing to fix this car reflected on me. I was worried about the money.

It turned out there was a scrap yard not far from our apartment. So every Saturday morning, I would go down to the scrap yard looking for any new arrivals. And every Saturday I would come home empty handed. After two months of looking and looking for that part and finding nothing, I started to worry. Not the "what am I going to eat for lunch" kind of worry, but the "this is going to ruin me" kind of worry. The inspection was upon me and I had nothing. And you need to know this was a major prayer request for me at the time.

With only a week to go, I decided to give it one last-ditch effort at the scrap yard. I tried for months and couldn't find what I needed, but with one week to go before the inspection, a nice little 1986 Honda Civic came in that was crumpled on the right side, but the left was in just fine condition.

So I pulled that fender off, paid the man, and carried it back to our apartment. I cried a little. Tears of joy. Tears because I realized in a very practical way that God was real, that He loves me, and that He literally showed up and provided that fender for me, and just in time. If I found the fender the first, or second, or even third time I went to the scrap yard, or if I had all the cash I needed to fix the car immediately, in either case, I would not have seen God's hand in this little detail of my life. I would have missed the very real intervention for good on my behalf by the Creator of the Universe.

My faith grew tremendously because of that experience and I have referenced that story to myself many times since then to remind myself that God provides what I need when I need it, despite what I might think.

Time would bring me much greater needs than a dented car fender, and I would question God more profoundly, and my faith. I have had to learn that lesson over and over again, in harder and harder ways. But that is our God. He never stops chasing after us and chipping away at the things that keep us from going all in for Him. When I read about Jesus saying that not even one hair will fall from our head without God knowing, I understood and agreed with the fact that He knows all. But I thought that maybe His motive in keeping track of us so closely was to make sure we're doing the right things. After I saw Him give me the car fender at just the right time I understood that He keeps track of us because He loves us and wants the best for us. He wants us to live, really live.

Years later I reflected back and I noticed something regarding those experiences with God. As my career (and income) took off, those real experiences seemed more like history than current events in my life. I didn't see the hand of God intervening in my life as much in real and tangible ways. I knew He was still with me, and I still followed Him but the tactile sense of God caring for me was more distant. We could now fix our car, rather *cars* (plural), as needed, put an addition on our house, take nice trips, etc., without much hesitation or financial concern. And we could shop at stores that we didn't really go to before. We didn't do much shopping, but I knew that if we wanted to shop we could go to the *nice* stores.

I think that is what happens, often, to people as life moves on. The stuff of life creeps up and blurs our vision and the memories of God's hand moving in our hearts and lives become faint and distant.

Life was getting more comfortable, but I longed for the real experience with God, the raw trust and love that I knew during those times. I wanted that again. And God wanted it for me too. If I'd known better, I'd have been a bit more worried.

FOUR
BALANCE

When Jaye and I started our life as a married couple together, I think I had my priorities as straight as they could be at 22 years old. I had the opportunity to interview with corporations and international organizations that may have taken me to different parts of the country and the world on a regular basis. But we were getting married, and I knew that traveling a lot and a good marriage are basically incompatible (sounds smart doesn't it? The truth is I couldn't stand the thought of being away from my new wife for that long). So we knew our family came first. I distinctly remember mapping out my day—I would spend 8 hours at work, 8 hours at home, and 8 hours sleeping, and I would achieve perfect balance. Ah, the naïveté of youth.

First of all, we lived in the metro Washington, D.C. area, which is not exactly easy to get around. I quickly realized that my commute amounted to 45 minutes each way in D.C. traffic, and if a squirrel ran in front of a sensitive animal lover on the beltway it could turn into a two-hour bottleneck. Then I was looking at an hour and a half, easy. Oh, and then I found out that the dress code for a banker was suit and tie every day, which took my fingers a while to adjust to (all those buttons and tie loops). That added at least 20 minutes to my prep time in the morning. So my 8 hours of private time was down to 6.

And then it hit me that they add an hour to your workday for lunch, even if I didn't need or want a whole hour. Down to 5. Five hours home with my wife every day. I guess I could deal with that. But that was the bare minimum.

I took a job as a management trainee with a large and very respected financial institution, where we were given all the best tools to be the most effective, successful, sales people and people managers in the business. We were given a sense of importance, by design, because we were "the future" of the company. A host of former trainees were brought in to speak to us, who had risen to great heights and were leaders in the Corporation now.

One of them told a trainee in private that he had wished he had gotten married later in life so he would have been less distracted professionally. I was already married before I started there, so I suppose that was a black mark on my record. At the end of the 9-month program, we were invited to the dining room of the top floor of the headquarters' main tower, where the CEO, CFO, COO, Big Cheese, Top Dogs, all sit, for an executive celebratory lunch. This was it; we were graduating from the program and were now expected to do great things.

I'm not sure when my priorities got fuzzy and confused. But at some point early on I decided I wanted to be the best. I wanted to be the best salesperson, exceed all the goals they gave me, get the best reviews, the biggest bonuses, the top raises. I wanted to be recognized for my achievements. It was middle and high school all over again, only it wasn't a letter jacket and trophies, it was money, sales trip awards, and recognition at corporate events that I was after. At the same time, however, I wanted to be a good husband, and good father to my future kids. I wanted to serve in our church and be a good friend. I wanted to be a successful and balanced person.

That's possible, isn't it?

When I was at the bank, I observed that there are the ones who pour their lives into their careers at the admitted expense of their relationships. They are usually the ones who end up on top and get the nod for the big job because they are willing to sacrifice for the company. But most of us want a good marriage, to be good parents, have some good friends, and be successful in our careers. We want to provide nice things for our families and have nice vacations. We may even want to be able to give some of it to church or charity.

We strive for success at work and at home. What's wrong with that?

The problem is that businesses, governments, churches, etc. are filled with men and women who might be "successful" but are miserable and broken. People who try to achieve "balance" between successful careers and successful private lives are usually anything but balanced. Rather, they are living muted lives. By trying to strike balance they achieve nothing of great value in the final accounting. They've bought into the lie that success is defined by a comfortable living, a planned retirement, decent house, nice car (or two), and to be respected by your peers. Some of these things might be more important than others to different people. But most of us have some mythical vision of "success" in our minds that makes us believe the lie of "balance."

Balance between two competing types of success is impossible.

It was after the training program was over that we moved to a small town, Harrisonburg, in the Shenandoah Valley of Virginia. That was where I would get my start on the ladder as a branch manager at one of the local branches. It was in the same town as JMU, our university, and the church we attended together while we dated, so it was like coming home. But I wasn't supposed to get my start there. I was supposed to come out of the gates in the metro-Washington D.C. area, the top division of the company. Somewhere in that first year of corporate life I got a glimpse of life on the corporate ladder in the fast-paced D.C. market and I envisioned much longer days and no time with my wife, and hopefully children down the road at some point.

It seemed that I knew myself and that I would probably have a hard time fighting the temptation to sacrifice my wife and family in the name of professional success. And how would I have the time I truly desired with my family? In the small university town where we fell in love and grew up spiritually, we had great friends and support. And there wasn't any traffic there. I thought I could regain an hour each day of my private time by working in a small town and living 10 minutes from the office. I was going for more balance. So at some career risk, I asked to be moved to the rural Virginia area because, as I told my superiors, it would be better for my family. And when they agreed to it, I felt that feeling you get when you know you've done something inherently good, something for God that flies in the face of the wisdom of the world. So we packed up and moved back to our university town.

Things went well and I was given bonuses and promotions. About a year later Jaye and I thought that we were in an ideal situation, so we bought our first house, settled on a hill over looking the Shenandoah Valley. Things couldn't have been better for a young couple. Our great friends, Joel and Teresa, lived only minutes away. Joel and Teresa "adopted" Jaye and I when we were in college through our church's "adopt-a-student" initiative, meant to link up lonely immature students like me with church families who live in the real world. Truly, they adopted me and then I asked if I could bring my girlfriend along. They were both in their twenties at the time but were younger in heart, enjoying the same playfulness Jaye and I did. And now we were two young couples living minutes apart, spending a lot of evenings and weekends together.

Big Steve, the man who introduced me to Jesus when I was 18 and mentored me all through college, was still there mentoring me spiritually. And our church was amazing, I mean amazing. A place where people were far from perfect, but knew they were forgiven by God's amazing grace, and who really wanted to love God and one another. A perfect spot for a Christian to raise his family, right? Give me time and I'll mess it up.

I looked up the corporate ladder in the small town and I realized that I would have to be in this small town a LONG time to achieve the success I wanted. So six months later I was applying for a promotion in Charlotte, NC, the headquarters of the bank. If I got the job, it would be a higher pay grade and a faster track up the ladder. I got that thrill you feel when you know something exciting is going to happen, like a promotion, a title, and a "relocation package." It wasn't the peaceful feeling that you get after you spend time praying, because I didn't pray much about it. I knew I wanted it, and I thought Jaye would come around to the idea. I called her up and asked her to meet me at a restaurant near my office so I could share the news.

"Jaye, I've got something to tell you. I'm thinking about applying for a job that will be the next step up in management."

"Ok. It's here in Harrisonburg, right?"

"Uh, well, it's actually in Charlotte."

"What? We just bought a house!"

"I know. I just don't know how much longer I can stay in this job? It'll take forever for me to get to the next level here. I mean, there are men here who have been in the same job for 20 years going nowhere fast."

"We just bought a house? I want to raise our kids here. We have great friends here and a great community."

"Jaye, it's important for me as a man to reach my potential. I can't just stay in this job forever."

"I'm not moving . . ."

(Silence)

We had an amazing friendship with Joel and Teresa in Harrisonburg. We spent 3 or 4 nights a week together, talking and laughing. They were our support system and we relied on them deeply. Our hearts were truly knit together. Greater friends you cannot find. We had an experience of great community with Joel and Teresa, and it was one that should have been high on the totem pole of priorities when considering a move to another state.

We were just starting to get involved in volunteer work with our church serving the huge Hispanic community where my Spanish speaking ability was proving to be very helpful. My career would move slowly though, most likely, given the lack of openings above me because people had the tendency to stay in their jobs until they died. I did some self-analysis and tried to make sure that my priorities were still intact. I decided that it would be a good balance for us in Charlotte because my extended family lived there and we heard that there was a good church that we could get plugged into.

Some very quiet days went by and my wife of great faith came back to me and said that she prayed a lot about it. Jaye told me that God had truly changed her heart and she supported me in what I felt I needed to do. I believe God did change her heart. Not because she needed changing, but because He had me on a path to learn something that would take years to learn and He knew that I would have to drag my loving wife along to learn it.

So six months after buying a house we thought we would raise our kids in, we stuck a for-sale sign in the yard, the relocation package kicked in, and we moved.

The new job in Charlotte was good and I excelled. As soon as I arrived, I was given a copy of the company's sales incentive plan, and I started doing the math and planning my income strategy. I started making sizable commissions and getting a taste of success. I even won a sales trip to a resort in the Caribbean. But I saw that my boss was making twice as much as me for my efforts. That was it. I had to have his job.

My heart was set on the next promotion. When I got it, I excelled, and started seeking the next one, and eventually got it as well. They made me a vice president and suddenly I was official. I had always said titles didn't matter, but I was lying. I was a vice president.

I was very impressed with myself. And I wanted others to be as well. I really did love it when people asked for my business card. You know the feeling? And the further up I went, my 5 hours of private time with my wife and Carter, our new baby girl, was down to 3, and often less. Evenings at work became more "necessary." And they gave me a computer at home so I could be more "efficient."

I was moving up and achieving success.

Our house was very nice for a young couple. But as our bank account grew, the house seemed smaller than when we bought it. So we built an addition off the back to give us more living space. Not long after we finished the addition I was surfing "online" (a new concept at the time) and found a custom-built home on 3 acres just minutes away. *Why not look at it?* I thought.

So we did. And we bought it.

Man, was it a nice house. There we were, 28 years old, in a giant, beautiful, secluded custom-built home nestled in 3 wooded acres in a major city, with a playhouse and a garden, and a private screened in porch off the gargantuan master bedroom. I had done it. I had achieved success and I could show it. My priorities were still there, not like when we first got married, but I still was focused on my wife and child. And I was a leader in our church where we were active in the youth group and missions. We had great friends. Life was good.

And that's how it happened.

I might have set out to have balance, with good priorities, but inevitably my desires for comfort, respect, nice things, and achievement, coupled with society's influence, crowded out my priorities, bit by bit, slowly or quickly, but it happened. I justified doing more, striving for more, buying more, sacrificing time at home away from family and friends and church, in the name of success.

I've seen it over and over again with friends and coworkers. Our idea of "balance" becomes "at least I'm home most weekends." And I could see myself as a committed church attendee who eventually justifies "having" to go into the office or meet a client on Sunday morning or afternoon.

My wife and I were trying to have another child to help fill the new house, when boom, that happened. She was pregnant with twins! Now, that's a scary proposition for any couple, but Jaye happens to have cystic fibrosis, a genetic lung disease, and diabetes. Adding a pregnancy with twins to that medical mix was, to say the least, daunting.

I remember the tender ultrasound nurse turning to Jaye and saying, "Honey, you got two of 'em in there." They say you can still hear the echo of my jaw hitting the shiny hospital floor.

So we looked up "ultra-high-risk-TO-THE-MAX OBGYNs" and found a great doctor, a wonderful Christian man who brought peace and faith to the room every time he entered it. Time went along and she got big, fast.

Then the real fun began.

I thought I was a man of faith who trusted God's providence in our lives because He loves us and had shown His care for us in specific ways in our lives in the past. Maybe it wasn't Uncle Jack sort of faith, but it was still real faith. When I saw Jaye begin to get bigger, and also slower, and then slower, and her body around the distended belly get thinner, and then thinner, I was terrified. Soon, we were going in and coming out of the hospital every week or so, and soon after, she had to be on oxygen 24/7. And in no time at all, I was in complete crisis mode.

I had a lot of stuff churning in my mind and heart at that time.

"What is going to happen here, Lord?"

"Is she going to make it through this?"

"Are my babies going to make it?"

"God, what exactly are you doing?"

With a lot of help, prayer, sleepless nights, and medical intervention, she made it through the pregnancy, and we arrived at the day of delivery.

While still struggling to get enough oxygen, she gave birth to a girl and a boy, 6 weeks premature.

Our daughter, Ayden, came first. She was small but strong without any major problems.

And then came Colson 8 minutes later. The nurses whisked him away and I could barely make out what he looked like, but I saw his sunken chest desperately trying to take in air, because his lungs weren't ready. We would have to wait in the delivery room for a couple of hours until we knew. Finally the neonatal doctor came in and told us about his lungs and a few other medical issues. She couldn't tell us he would be all right, because she didn't know.

Early the next morning we were able to go down and see the babies. First Ayden, so small but so alive. We held her briefly and it was wonderful. Then we went to the intensive care side to see our son. What an awful sight of tubes and monitors coming out of a 4-pound baby. I couldn't hold him, but I could reach inside the incubator with the built-in rubber gloves to touch him. I had no words. All I could do was pray, "God, please heal him".

Just then his former-nun-turned-nurse piped in, "Don't worry Dad, he's just a wimpy white-boy."

Not exactly comforting words, but apparently in neonatal ICU wards they label white boy babies because they're usually the worst cases, the slowest to get in shape.

And there he stayed, week after week. The updates from the doctors were "cautiously optimistic," but they were not sure that everything would be "ok" and it was clear in their voices.

Suddenly the big house, the great career, the success didn't mean much to me. And my faith was shaking like a leaf in late October.

I still believed that God was real and well aware of our situation, but did I trust Him? Did I believe that "all things work together for good for those who love Him?" (Rom 8:28). Did I believe He loved me? I didn't know. But I prayed, and my good friend Jeff was there all the time talking and praying with me. A friend who comes along once, maybe twice, in a lifetime, if you're lucky.

Finally Colson began to turn the corner, and his lungs progressed. The ventilator came out and so did the tubes. After 7 agonizing weeks he was ready to come home.

So there we were, a family of 5. Jaye and I played two-on-one defense for 2 years but had to go right to the zone. Jaye started getting her health and strength back and things started getting back to normal. I was able to get back into stride at work. But something was different.

I had seen God work again in our lives and I walked away with a more abiding faith that I could trust Him, that He was faithful to my family and me. My faith was even stronger, I think.

But my character hadn't changed a bit.

It didn't take too long before a job opening caught my eye in another state. I saw the job posting for a position that would be a monumental jump in my career with much greater responsibility and clout. And money . . . a lot of money. In fact, I thought, there would be plenty of money to pay a full-time nanny to cover for me because I would have to be on the road most of the time. Think of the life we could have? And think of the respect I would garner?

A regional director at 29? Unheard of.

The state director flew me in for an interview, along with several other candidates. After the interview day, I was the top candidate. So his assistant called me the next day and said that he would be flying in at 8:00 the next morning to spend the day watching me in action. And so he did.

But it was clear we were oil and water. It didn't work out.

After the excitement and rush of the interviewing process was over and it was clear I wasn't going to be offered the job, my mind settled and I had time to think. At first I was mad that this guy didn't recognize the obvious brilliance I could offer. But then it turned into reflection. Reflection over what I had almost done.

Here I was, the father of 3 children under 3 years old, all in diapers, a wife who needs me around to help out because of her health more than most wives need their husbands, and I was a millimeter away from moving them to another state, hiring a nanny to farm out my parental responsibilities, and never seeing them because I would be working all the time. What had I almost done?

Coming out of the experience with Jaye and the twins, I had a renewed sense of devotion to my family and appreciation of life and the gifts God gives. When the regional director position caught my eye, it wasn't as if my true love for my family went out the window. Rather, I justified my motives for wanting the promotion with a list of false benefits to my family.

We could be back at our old church, we could be closer to Jaye's sister Kim and our great friends, it's a better area to raise our children, I would have more money to give to God's work, etc. But the truth of it was that I envisioned my name on a short list of people holding that position, the excitement of business travel, the amount of influence, and a lot of money. The downside didn't seem so down, and the upside seemed sky high, for me.

But that's just it; it was for me

- not because I felt God wanted it for me,
- not because it was truly best for my family,
- not because I could have more time to help people around me,
- not because it would be an opportunity for me to grow more in faith, hope, and love.

It was none of that, because none of that would have happened had I been given that job. Had they offered it to me I would have taken it, that's for sure. And I would have been an absentee dad, with a practically abandoned wife, and a church pew sitter, when I was home to make it to church.

God rescued me again. He rescued me from climbing a ladder of success that would have left me and my family leaning against a paper wall that time and pressure would eventually cause to fall. When I got the news that I didn't get the job, I knew it was God intervening in my life again. But this time something drastic had happened in my heart and mind. I got a glimpse of the deadly combination of the seduction of success and selfishness. It scared me how willing I was to drink it up and how adept I was at finding selfless sounding reasons to justify the decision.

It was then that the course of my life, my concept of faith, and my understanding of God's purpose all drastically changed.

FIVE
SLOGANS

When I landed my first position as a manager, my boss gave me this little book with an eagle on the cover soaring over the crest of a snow-covered mountain. I still have it in my office downstairs. It's a compilation of slogans, or inspirational quotes. Why is it that so many of us like a good slogan? "Shoot for the moon. Even if you miss, you'll land among the stars," or "Live for the day," or how about this one: "Success is not a destination, it's a journey." There are entire books filled with inspirational slogans to help us strive for our best. I have a shelf full of them that I collected in corporate life. I would love to tell you that I never cracked those books, but that would be a lie. I read them, and at times I read them a lot. Really now, what would cause me to feel the need to draw some motivation from printed sound bites from people I don't know? Good question.

Where do those slogans come from? They are not derived from people you've never heard about, otherwise why should we listen? But if Dale Carnegie, Bill Gates, Teddy Roosevelt, or Donald Trump say something, you better believe that someone is going to hang on to every word, condense it into a catch phrase, and come up with a slogan that millions of people can be inspired by. In other words, those life slogans, those inspirational mottoes, come from *successful* people, people whose achievements represent the life we think we want, who have the things we think we need, who don't seem to have the problems we have.

I can honestly say that I have no recollection of reading or caring about any motivational quote until I was out of college and in a career. What I do remember in high school is Stuart Smalley staring into a mirror and telling himself, "I'm good enough, I'm smart enough, and dogone it, people like me." I think I actually tried that a few times in my bedroom. That was about as close as I came to self-motivating affirmations. That's when I had a *lot* of time to idealize about what my role in this planet should be, how I was going to lead the masses, invent the painless dental floss, heal the planet, etc. Those precious late teen, early twenties years are full of vision for the future, visions of personal greatness, and how our lives are limitless. We know exactly what our lives should be about and what we should accomplish. *Then* we graduate, and our idealism clashes with the reality that life is hard and it takes a lot of work.

Looking back, I see some commonalities between my friends in high school and college and me, at least enough to draw some conclusions. The pattern looks something like this: Coming out of college we interview with companies or institutions that we think will put us on the path toward success, get knocked down a few times, and then land that first job. It isn't exactly what we had in mind, but we know if we just apply ourselves, work hard, dress snappy, learn the lingo and all the acronyms, latch onto the right person that's a rung or two ahead of us on the ladder, then we will achieve success. And then weeks turn into months, and months into years, of the same old thing, day in and day out, and the fire for success becomes harder to stoke.

But someone up the ladder is smart enough to give you "Secrets of Success: Quotes to Inspire" to re-stoke the fire for success in you. You pour through and find "You cannot sit on the road to success, if you do you'll get run over." That does it. That's exactly the slogan you needed to inspire you to pull yourself up and get back on that road to success. You print it out in huge font and paste it to your cubicle wall. You start getting to work early, cutting lunch short, staying late, and going to all the right company "events" (opportunities to schmooze the guys on the upper rungs).

That's why I sat in my office at times and read my little slogan book. I wanted to be great. I wanted to be successful. And I was starting to realize that it doesn't come easy. Success required work and time and energy, but so did being a good husband to Jaye and father to my children. Success is hard; life is hard. But deep down striving to succeed was beginning to seem a bit futile to me. When those little thoughts of clarity began to creep in when I was staring down my sales goals or sitting in a managers meeting, I had to stamp them out because they are inherently dangerous to the path to "excellence." That is when the slogan book gets whipped out. Slogans were anesthesia to cover the pain in my heart that the truth left me with. They distracted me from the realization of the futility of it all and helped me "re-focus."

During and after the pregnancy and birth of the twins, I was deeply engaged in major self-reflection and searching mode. Someone up the food chain at the company must have noticed that I wasn't the guy I was before. They must have concluded that I needed something. They were smart enough to invite me to a "success seminar," with some top-notch successful people to explain how they became successful, and the secret ingredients needed on the road to success.

If you haven't been to one of these, this is how it went. The seminar had a pre-reading program to help you get your mind ready to absorb the greatness of the seminar speakers. When I got there with the other weighed-down, burned out employees, the convention center was perfectly lit for maximum motivation, blaring the theme song from Rocky III, "Eye of the Tiger." The emcee walked out with perfect hair in a perfect suit (who probably has the perfect wife and car and bank account) to introduce us to the first speaker, who started from nothing, set definite goals, worked hard, took calculated risks, and found success in the world of internet technology. The second speaker walked out on stage and told us the same thing, only he did it in sales. The third had exactly the same story, only he made millions by inventing whiter teeth or something. I started getting the picture: If I set definite goals, work hard, and take calculated risks, I too can have perfect hair, the perfect suit, a great car, and bank account. Now you may not actually tell anyone that you want what the speakers have, but that's surely what you are after. And that's what the guys up the rungs on the ladder want you to have, because that helps them get it too (only more of it).

That's what it's all about right?

I was struggling with what my life was all about, what my purpose was. I picked up the slogan book from time to time and found other deeper, more purposeful mottoes from people like Helen Keller; quotes like, "I long to accomplish a great and noble task, but it is my chief duty to accomplish small tasks as if they were great and noble." That resonated with me and I would try to bring meaning to my life and work, but, if I were being honest, really I wanted the nice house, the respectable car, the respect of others, and bragging rights. And this was ultimately proven by my actions. I might have said all the right things and I might have even been able to quote Helen Keller or the Bible, but my actions proved my motives.

The idea of success is something that was born in me and something that was driven into me throughout my entire life. Our natures are such that we want to reward ourselves and have comfort, luxury, or respect, and the world around us encourages us to want those things for ourselves. I really don't need the world to tell me to strive to take care of myself; we have plenty of that drive born within us. But the combination of our natural desires and the marketing of society provide a formidable enemy to the very things that we will all want in the end. I'm convinced that we will all lie on our deathbed and have either the satisfaction of a life well spent or regret for a life spent on us.

I'm convinced now that in the end my life, and all lives, will be rendered empty without love, joy, peace, patience, kindness, goodness, faithfulness, gentleness, and self-control, the qualities the Bible calls the "fruit of the Spirit" (Gal 5). I believe that if I don't have those things permeating my life and relationships then I will be void, and will be painfully aware of my emptiness. It is sad to me because it seems that most people only seem to understand that later in life, after they've spent their lives striving for success. Maybe a lot of people strive for success at home and success at work, and maybe in some cases there are people who can pull that off. By God's grace, and not because I figured it out on my own, I realized that my heart was set on trying to balance success at home and at work. I wanted both. But God was about to make it abundantly clear to me that it doesn't work that way. I was about to come to the shocking realization that it isn't about "balancing" work "success" and home "success". It's about turning the entire idea of success upside down.

SIX
ECONOMICS

What caused me to interview for the director position? Was it a desire for security? Did I feel that it was the responsible thing to do to use the gifts God has given me to the fullest possible potential? "God made me a good manager of people, so I should use those gifts as much as possible," I thought. Kind of an Eric-Little-in-Chariots-of-Fire, "God-made-me-fast" thing. Or maybe, deep down, I wanted people to think highly of me at church and at my 20-year high school reunion. This was before Facebook and Twitter where I could brag about myself on a daily basis. All of that might have been some of what was in my heart and mind.

But what it came down to was that I wanted the highest level of success. Success meant respect, the ability to hold my chin up and say what I do for a living out loud at parties. Success meant that my parents could brag about me to their friends and relatives. And yes, it meant money. Success meant making a lot of money. That's the way it works. I wanted to be successful, and the most successful I could be. I still wanted to be a good husband, father, friend, and church member. But I wanted to be successful too. Actually, I observed that almost all the men given leadership roles at church were successful in their careers, had nice houses and cars, so wanting to be like them was actually a holy thing, right?

Some years before I was asked to teach a Sunday school class on Christian finances. Because I was a banker they figured I knew something about money, apparently more than the skillful science of giving people money and making them pay it back with interest. I knew all or most of the major Bible references about money. I knew all about the ant in Proverbs who saves in summer for the cold in winter. Or if you want to build a tower, you had better sit down and make a good plan and count the costs, or you will look like a fool (Luke 14:28-30). Jaye and I had studied "Christian finances" in our premarital counseling, which did a lot to help us understand about budgeting, living within your means, and the rules of compound interest. And here I was teaching Sunday school on how to save for emergencies, invest in a 401k, make a budget, and the most effective way to cut up credit cards.

There was one thing that Jesus said that really gnawed at me though: "No one can serve two masters. He'll either hate one and love the other, or he will be devoted to one and despise the other. You cannot serve both God and money." (Matt 6:24). I couldn't wrap my mind completely around that one. Our parents raise us to work hard and dream big, and of course they want us to be successful. What parent wants their children to be un-successful? But what did God think of my desire for success? "He will either hate the one and love the other . . . You cannot serve both God and money." I began to pray, "God, what do I do with this? What does it mean to hate money?"

What is it about human nature that makes us lust for money? Now, don't get me wrong, I don't think most people run around with daggers in their pockets ready to slash someone for some cash, but I do think there is a strong general desire among us to accumulate. I've traveled to several other countries and have studied the cultures and economic systems of many others, namely in Latin America. Compared to every other culture I've experienced, the general culture of the United States has a much higher degree of desire for accumulating things. This country has produced a greater amount of wealth than any other nation at any other time in history, which, I believe, can be attributed to the truly unmatchable freedom that its people enjoy. The wealth we enjoy is a great blessing, and because our citizens, as a whole, are the most generous in the world, our wealth has been used to bless the world. That is a wonderful thing and we should celebrate that fact. But I think that the demonstration of wealth has stirred in us a lust for more. I see it in the immigrant families with whom I work and are part of my church. The first generation immigrants are truly thankful just to have a job that pays them and roof over their heads, and maybe a 12 year old used car to get them to work. To be able to send their kids to a good school and have paved roads is like heaven. They know what they came from, and this is paradise comparatively. But their children don't know what their parents came from. As much as their parents try to explain it to them, all they know is that they are poor, and that the other kids in school have cars and X-Boxes and iPhones, and they want it all. The American Dream of a decent living and a piece of land has turned into the hottest car and latest gadgets.

I was making more money than I ever expected at my age, but God started to open my eyes to a few things about wealth. Wealth was producing not a bit of character improvement in me. I could see that wealth might buy me good schools for our kids, which might teach good morals, but it will not buy me character as a father. I had a comfortable life, but I had less peace in my heart and more worry. We were able to take trips to Europe and Caribbean resorts with money, but none of that produced lasting joy. Having money wasn't solving the problem of my impatience and anger. I had friends from work who saw me as a gravy train because I had success, but money didn't buy me lasting, true friendships with them. You can try to buy your friends, but when the gifts stop, so do the good times with your buddies. I know that one from experience.

Jesus made a profound statement when He taught about the impossibility of serving both God and money. We have all at least heard that verse. But the most recognizable part of the verse is "you cannot serve both God and money," because it's easy to say that we don't serve money, because, after all, we go to church and serve in the youth ministry or choir or maybe even leadership. But what about Jesus' statement that you will either hate God and love money, or you will hate money and love God? Jesus really didn't mean that did he? I mean, we may not *love* money, but we don't hate it. We just really, really *like* having it. But Jesus said if you love God then you must hate money. It's not ambiguous. But maybe this was one of Jesus' hyperboles, right? Like when he said if your eye causes you to sin, pluck it out. He was just demonstrating the severity of the sin and the extent we should go to in order to avoid it, right?

Can't I love God and be neutral about money, maybe even like it a little? That's what I thought.

Unfortunately, we hear the same message from many of the fast-growing evangelical churches today. "God wants you to be healthy and wealthy" is the mantra. Man, if I didn't know God's word then I would absolutely be attracted to that message. God was changing me and opening my eyes to what was really in my heart, what the world is really like, and what true life really is. My heart was split open during the experience with the twins and God poured Himself into it. He was teaching me not that He wants me to be healthy and wealthy, rather that He wants me to literally and practically trust Him daily, in everything, for everything.

When I was in college, early in my faith, I confided in Big Steve about the anxiety I experienced on a daily basis. He saw that worry was like a ball and chain tied to my leg that I had to drag around everywhere I went. I worried about the future, about relationships, about failure. Steve helped me learn to turn to Scripture to find what God has to say about each issue of life. So I turned to Matthew 6: 25-34 and saw Jesus telling His disciples, "Do not worry about your life" and "can any of you by worrying add a single hour to your life?" I saw His command, but that was like telling me not to breathe.

Worry was a part of life for me, like a bad splinter in my foot that I couldn't dig out. I knew that at its core was a lack of trust in God as my Father, but I couldn't overpower the worry. But then I read at the end of this passage Jesus saying that we don't need to chase after things; things like food, drink, and clothing. I think He was telling His friends in their context to not spend their lives worrying about getting the things they think they need to be comfortable. Then Jesus said, "But seek first His Kingdom and His righteousness, and all these things will be given to you as well." For years these words of Jesus were in the forefront of my mind, as an abstract goal that I couldn't practically decipher. I couldn't understand what exactly it meant to "seek first His Kingdom and His righteousness".

During one spring break in college, Big Steve invited me and a group of guys to travel to Atlanta, GA to spend 6 days with a man named Bob Lupton. Bob was a successful businessman who lived in the affluent suburbs of Atlanta, but had a real desire to mentor inner city kids who didn't have many opportunities. On Saturdays he would travel downtown and would meet with kids to try to help them and teach them about Jesus. Over time he grew more and more distressed over leaving these kids in their dilapidated living conditions and poverty and returning to his suburban home. He became so convicted and so full of compassion that he bought a run-down house in the middle of a tough, drug-infested, neighborhood in downtown Atlanta, and moved his family there. He began to live among the people he wanted to serve, to bring redemption to their lives and their neighborhood. We spent a week with Bob and his ministry, taking in the beauty of the effects of one man taking seriously the call to seek first the Kingdom.

A few times during the week we had debriefing sessions with Bob. His radical lifestyle change for the sake of the Kingdom was shocking and inspiring. But what was equally shocking was his view on money, which I can see now corresponds perfectly to his view on our responsibility in seeking the Kingdom first. He didn't save money, and didn't worry at all about it. He worked to build sustainable income and to teach others to be entrepreneurial, but he didn't plan a 5-year financial course. He trusted God. And he believed that when Jesus said, "Do not store up treasure on earth" that He meant it, simply and clearly.

Some of the more well versed students of the bible then asked him about Solomon's teaching in Proverbs 6:6-8 that we should save up for winter because that is the wise thing to do. I will never forget Bob Lupton's response.

"Jesus said, 'Look at the lilies of the field and how they grow. They don't work or make their clothing. Yet Solomon in all his glory was not dressed as beautifully as they are'." And then he just looked at us in silence, letting the message soak in and permeate our hearts and minds. The clear message that Bob was giving us was that Jesus' way was a better way, that trusting the Father is more important than any wise plan we may have. It struck me that it was exactly this point that gave him the desire and power to radically seek the Kingdom.

After I didn't get the "big job" I was reflecting again on Jesus' words to "seek first His Kingdom." Like looking through a blurry camera lens of a beautiful landscape that was slowly coming into focus, I was beginning to see what He meant. I think He was telling me to not spend my life focused on chasing after the things I think want, or even the things I think I need. In my modern context, I think He was telling me not to spend my life worrying about accumulating things like money, a house, a comfortable retirement nest-egg, health insurance, life insurance, cars, etc. I was focused on accumulating things, things that I felt my family and I needed, things that I feared losing if I didn't succeed. I was focused first on working hard, and then in my spare time to work for God.

This "seek first" thing wasn't a reality to me. In my reality, it was more like "seek second" after I take care of my necessities. It clearly wasn't a command for just pastors and missionaries, it was for all His followers. So how then do I seek His Kingdom first in my life, in my context? I was beginning to see what it meant.

I looked again at all of the books on "Christian finances" and compared them with Jesus' teaching on not worrying about money, storing up treasure in heaven not on earth, trusting in the Father for our "daily bread," selling our possessions if they were possessing us, and His warnings against the deceitfulness of wealth. The books on Christian finances I read were great in teaching about living within a budget, giving tithes, and not going into debt for things we can't pay for. I also found that most of those books talked all about the wisdom of saving for emergencies and retirement. But I couldn't find any of the major writers and experts stressing above all other things that God wants our hearts more than our money, He wants us to trust Him as our Father. They didn't tell me that even if I am tithing and could afford it in my budget, spending money so that I'm essentially living for myself and broadcasting my wealth to my neighbors was probably not God-honoring. The success stories of people who had graduated from their program were all about how they thanked God because before the program they were full of anxiety, but now had peace in their lives because they now have 6 months of income in a bank account and $25,000 in their 401k. I was a poster boy for the Christian finance gurus, but I didn't practically trust God for my daily bread.

Something seemed to be off in my life.

Early in my faith, a good friend exposed me to the music of Keith Green. Now if you don't like to be challenged and have your conscience pricked a little, then don't listen to Keith Green. I loved his music, consuming it constantly like food. Keith was so bold and direct, and throughout his music you find a challenge to really live the life laid out for us by Jesus in His word, in a radical way. But as I looked at my life years later, I wasn't living up to that notion of radical living. I loved the theory, but was scared of the practice.

Now I was changing. God was changing me. I wanted to live.

My wonderful father-in-law is a great poker player, and I, like a fool bent on losing money, have attempted to play with him more than once. I love when he toys with the other players through a hand, and then, towards the end, he says, "All in." That means if you want to play then you have to put every last chip you have in. You can't keep any chips "just in case." You can't hold any in reserve in case you have a bad hand. You have to put it all in.

Well I wanted to go "all in" for Jesus.

I wanted to cut the umbilical cord to finding security in the things that seemed to sustain me but were actually sucking the very life out of me. I thought I was living well, comfortable and balanced, careful and conservative, but it was not living, because ultimately it was for me, for my ego, for my legacy, my security, and all within my control. That's not real life; it's milquetoast living, the kind that isn't hot or cold. It's sour to the taste, and I knew Jesus would spit it right out of his mouth. I wanted to spit it out too.

I could no longer go on the way things were.

I knew that if I wanted to really live life in the Kingdom of God then I needed to open my eyes to what His economy is all about. I began to see that His economy is not the economy of the USA or the world. His economy is upside down. In our economy, the winner has the best job, the most respect, and the most money. But in God's economy the first will be the last, and the last will be first. He said that the greatest among you would be the least of all, the one who is the greatest servant of others, who gives up all for the sake of others.

In our economy, the leader is the one who commands the most attention and focus. In God's economy the leader is the one who is most patient and kind and who listens the most.

In our economy, the one who crosses the finish line first is the winner. In God's Kingdom, the one who makes sure everyone else is over the finish line first is the winner.

In our world, the one who can speak most eloquently in public is the most revered. The one who stacks the chairs so that everyone else can listen to the speaker is the most revered in God's economy.

In our economy, investing your money for a good retirement is wisdom. In God's economy, money and things are not wealth, but building up the faith, hope, and love of the people around you is eternal wealth. In God's economy faithfulness in trusting Him and depending on Him for the bread, milk, and eggs you need for each day is wisdom.

What then is a successful person in God's economy? He began to show me what a successful person is in His eyes, and that life didn't match up, no matter how much Bible knowledge I had, or my titles at work or at church. He showed me that a successful person, in God's eyes, is a person who does not worry about their life. That means they trust that God will provide for them and their family what they need—period. That no matter what, God will provide what they need. They don't need to worry about tomorrow because He promised to provide for today. That means they don't need to worry about money. And because God provides all that they have, they are careful to use what He gives wisely and not buy a lot of frivolous stuff. And because God will provide, that person doesn't need to strive to accumulate more and more and more in fear that some catastrophe will happen.

The successful person trusts his Father to provide.

A successful person in God's eyes is one who loves, truly loves, other people. First, his wife, or her husband, his children, his friends, his parents, his neighbors, strangers, and his enemies. He is patient, and kind, and isn't jealous of what they have that he doesn't have, doesn't brag about himself or what he has, because God is the one who gave the gifts in the first place. He isn't rude and selfish all the time, looking to interject himself in every conversation. He looks for ways to build other people up, and doesn't tear them down. He isn't proud about himself because he knows that God loves him and he doesn't need to make sure others know all his qualities out of a sense of insecurity. When people do or say bad things to him, he forgives them and might even sincerely pray for them. When they do it again, he forgives again, and again and again. When he does or says bad things to others he is quick to recognize his failing and asks for forgiveness. And this love for others doesn't have a time limit and isn't based on feelings, which come and go.

A successful person, in God's economy, is actively engaged in the lives of others, so much that when a need arises in someone's life he is there to offer a helping hand, time in and time out. And if his desires and priorities conflict with the needs of others, he'll work to find a way to help. This person doesn't have to be asked to help usually because he's aware of the needs. The football game or TV show are patently unimportant when a friend is there; he can enjoy them some other time because his friend is in the house.

A successful person looks to give away as much as he can to help the church, and gives at least a tenth, before taxes. He works to give to the poor and needy as much as possible.

A successful person is one who wants to honor God in all he says, does, thinks, and feels. That means he wants to be like Jesus, not like the coolest thing out of Hollywood. He wants to talk to Him, to listen to Him, to sing to Him, to see Him work in the lives of friends and neighbors, and he wants to follow His standards.

Does this sound like an angel or some heavenly being? Maybe it's impossible. Maybe it's only Jesus who can live that way. I thought that once, but now I see it's not impossible. This is exactly what God wants from us. God wants us to be successful in His economy and He gives us the power to live successful lives, to be good and faithful servants of the King.

When the Bible talks about the truth that God has freed His children, it means that He has freed us from the inability to live this way, and offers us the power to live successful lives in His Kingdom. It's not about being perfect and earning God's love. It's about really living life, passionate, joyful, full life, by His grace and His power. In God's Kingdom, people hate money. They hate the need for it, they hate what the desire for it does to relationships, they hate the fear of losing it because that exposes their lack of faith in their Father, and they long for the day when it will be totally and completely unnecessary in heaven.

It is true that we cannot serve both God and money.

I had to take a hard look at my heart and my life, and consider my level of trust in God as my Father, and make a sober judgment. When it came down to it, was I trying to serve both God and money? Was I trying to be successful in the Kingdom of God and the Kingdom of this world at the same time?

SEVEN
CRAZY

I remember like it was yesterday.

Jaye and I were sitting on our porch swing smelling the beautiful magnolia blooms on an incredible day. We were swinging while we looked out over the back yard of our beautiful house. Our twins were just babies and we were still in the throws of the feedings and diapers and naps. Over the past few weeks we had been talking and praying about crawling way out on a limb spiritually, emotionally, and financially, and then cutting it off behind us.

Through the whole experience of Jaye's pregnancy with the twins, then Colson's struggle, then the interview, I saw clearly that God wanted me to stop trying to be successful by the world's standards, but to strive to be successful in the Kingdom. He wanted me to start to truly trust Him as my Father who cares for my little family and me. I saw that this call wasn't just for pastors or missionaries, but it was for everyone, including me. I envisioned a life of truly believing the promises of God, of real, practical, daily faith. I wanted that because I knew it was the only real human life, the life God designed for us. I could sense God taking my hands in His, my hands that even then were clenched around my savings accounts, insurance plans, 401k, and stock options, and opening them finger by finger until these things that gave me false security were held loosely. I saw him gently passing His fingers across my face, teaching me to close my eyes so I wouldn't look ahead to try to plan for every circumstance. He was giving me a glimpse of what real life could be; the life of faith. And my faith had grown in a radical way. Faith that He would literally provide for our *daily* needs, including health insurance, a house, food, transportation, etc.

I wanted that faith, but I didn't have it yet.

As long as I had a paycheck I felt I wouldn't know what it was to trust God as my provider. But here I was with my family of 5; Jaye and her health needs, and my babies. Colson hadn't been off oxygen for very long and it was still unknown what his long-term health concerns would be. There was so much unknown. But did I believe God or not? In my mind, it was either true, or it wasn't.

A former coworker of mine, a good friend, Danny, left the bank a year or two before this time to start a mortgage business. While I was in the middle of trying to figure out God's specific will for me and for my family, I stopped by one day to visit my friend. I shared with him what we had been going through and how God had been stirring me up.

Danny is a great listener. About a week later a book showed up in the mail from an "anonymous" giver. The book was *Wild at Heart* by John Eldredge, and I poured myself into it instantly. I knew right away it was from Danny. He cared enough about me to send me this book that he knew would help me.

The book talks about a lot of things about men, but what struck me deeply was the fact that God made men "wild at heart," meaning that He made me to live radically with adventure, spirit and passion. But somewhere along the line I got sucked into the notion that I need to be tame and nice, and that I should plan out every aspect of our lives, in the most ordered fashion possible.

I wasn't living a passionate life, but I could sense that God was calling me to do just that.

I began thinking about farmers and hunters. Since the beginning of the world, men have been farmers and hunters. For thousands of years, the vast majority of men and their families provided their sustenance through tilling soil, planting seed, nurturing plants, harvesting, raising livestock, and hunting animals. It is a very recent occurrence in the history of man that so many rely upon a corporate or government paycheck to pay for their needs.

Thinking through the entire process of farming, it occurred to me that a lot of farmers must be people of great faith in God. They cultivate the land, plant, and harvest, but beyond that it is entirely out of their control. The crops need the right amount of sun and the right amount of rain to grow, and at any time pests could attack the plants and ruin everything. Only God can provide the heat, water, and protection necessary to produce a crop. Even if most farmers weren't followers of Jesus, they had to recognize that much of their success was out of their hands.

When Christian farmers read Jesus' instruction on how to pray, "Give us this day our daily bread," they must have understood the reality and necessity of that prayer. It wasn't an abstract concept of faith, but a real, daily prayer to God to provide food. I can imagine when they read Jesus' words, "Don't worry about tomorrow" and "look at the birds of the air, they neither toil or reap or gather into barns. Yet your heavenly Father feeds them. Are you not of more value than these?" (Matt 6:26), that must have made them feel secure like a child in his daddy's lap.

Should we be any different than the farmers? The human heart hasn't changed one iota since the beginning, but certainly our circumstances have. As technology has advanced so has efficiency in production and services, which produced immense wealth across wide swaths of society and the standard of living in the western world has risen exponentially. We are surrounded by wealth. Wealth can numb us to our need for God, who, despite our corporate paychecks and social security payments, is the provider of our needs. When we are comfortable in our bank accounts and careers, our 401k's and our life insurance plans, our hearts can be lured away from passionately relying upon our Father, who wants us to rely upon Him for everything. We can settle for a type of reliance that is anemic because it's all we know. We must make decisions that are based on putting us on the path of success in the Kingdom of God, not worrying about our comfort.

I now found myself in a place where I truly believed that God does provide for His children, that He literally enters into time and space and intervenes on our behalf to provide what we need, when we need it. It wasn't my skill or ability that sustained my family, but the grace and generosity of God that gave me and my family breakfast, lunch, dinner, health insurance, gas for my car and the car itself. And yes, I still wanted to be successful. Only now I felt a passion for success in the Kingdom stirring in me.

I wanted my life to be useful to my Savior and for His purposes.

Once I saw that it wasn't the management of a company that determined my well-being, or a corporate pension plan, or my 401k, but it was my Father who controls all things, then I realized how much I didn't like my job (funny how that works). And I drew a simple conclusion: The more successful I was at the bank, the more time I had to give them. When I achieved a promotion I was paid more money, given better stock options and more vacation time. In return I was expected to do more, to give more of myself. I was given more responsibilities and higher goals. The higher I climbed, the more money and prestige I garnered, the more stuff I accumulated, the harder it was to leave it. All of that time at work meant time away from home, time that I couldn't spend with my wife, my children, my family, my friends, and my neighbors.

On the other hand, if I found something that I could do for myself that would earn enough money, then in theory I wouldn't be a slave to hours at work.

Another coworker of mine had left the bank to start a business in real estate investing. After spending hours talking with him extensively about his business and studying the model, I felt that I could do the same thing. It seemed that it was possible to make enough money to pay our bills without it monopolizing my life. We carefully thought through the details. "But can I do this?" I wondered.

I remembered a song I heard on our road trip to visit Bob Lupton in college that just stuck in my head. It was a song on one of those Scripture memory albums meant to burn the verse on your brain. I still know the cheesy reggae tune, so it must have worked. "Trust in the Lord with all your heart, and lean not on your own understanding" (Proverbs 3:5-6) were the lyrics that made their way into my permanent memory.

And here I was ready to really trust in God for the details of my life and my future, and my families' future. It's up to me to make wise decisions, but ultimately He will provide. It was settled for me. We were going to do it. It meant leaving a successful career behind, along with its sweet benefits, closing my eyes and taking the hand of God.

I was ecstatic and terrified at the same time.

Then the question of where I would start the business came up, since I didn't want to impose on my friend's business by becoming a direct local competitor. Our good friends Jeff and Cami, who helped us sacrificially through the pregnancy and birth of the twins, had moved to Florida some months before. Jaye and I considered the life we're called to in the Kingdom and it was clear to us that it is a life of living in intentional community. A life where we are close emotionally with our like-minded friends, but also close in proximity. It's hard to live in community, real community, when you live 5 miles apart (I found that email, text and cell phones don't replace human eye contact and touch). We visited our friends in Florida and were sitting around after a meal and putting the kids to bed, when Cami said, "Wouldn't it be great if you were just next door?"

That casual question planted a seed, and the seed took root.

So there we were, sitting on our porch swing, overlooking our beautifully landscaped private back yard, discussing what the rest of our lives would look like. I knew there were several areas in which I wanted to be successful, but I knew that our current path was not the one on which we would find that success. We dreamed about a life where I must trust God to provide for our family but be able to spend as much time as possible with Jaye and the kids, and where, if a need arose among friends or neighbors (the biblical term for anyone I come across) that I would be able to help. We talked among our friends at church so much about the concept of living in community that we began making plans to reunite with our good friends in Florida so we could practice real community.

So we looked around, thought about what lasts and what's important and said, "It's only a house."

EIGHT
SELL

Just recently I read about an Austrian man, Karl Rabeder, who became a multi-millionaire in the home furnishings business. By the age of 47 he had acquired a villa with lake, sauna and spectacular mountain views over the Alps, valued at $2.2 million, a beautiful old stone farmhouse in Provence with its 17 hectares overlooking the Arrière-Pays, a collection of six gliders valued at $550,000, and a luxury Audi A8, worth around $69,000.

But this is what he had to say about all that: "For a long time I believed that more wealth and luxury automatically meant more happiness," he said. "I come from a very poor family where the rules were to work more to achieve more material things, and I applied this for many years." But over time, he had another, conflicting feeling. "More and more I heard the words: 'Stop what you are doing now—all this luxury and consumerism—and start your real life,'" he said. "I had the feeling I was working as a slave for things that I did not wish for or need."*

This man experienced a great revelation that few experience. He rose to the mountaintop of worldly success and he didn't have to climb it anymore. He looked around and found it empty and worthless. The

---

* "Millionaire gives away fortune that made him miserable," Telegraph.co.uk, Henry Samuel, Feb 2010.

problem with most of the rest of us is that we never really get to the top, but we *think* that we can achieve some semblance of success, and get a piece of the mountaintop, and we spend our lives chasing after that dream.

Mr. Rabeder continued sharing what happened to him on a lavish vacation to Hawaii: "It was the biggest shock in my life, when I realized how horrible, soulless and without feeling the five star lifestyle is," he said. "In those three weeks, we spent all the money you could possibly spend. But in all that time, we had the feeling we hadn't met a single real person—that we were all just actors. The staff played the role of being friendly and the guests played the role of being important and nobody was real."

What honest insight into a world we think we want, if *we* are honest. I don't think most people let themselves overtly want the 5-star lifestyle, because it is simply unattainable, and to overtly want the unattainable would drive you mad. But we would like to taste it, even in small ways. How do we do that? We buy the nicest things we can according to our socioeconomic level and within the standards of our peer group. That way compared to our peers we'll be at least "keeping up." And if we don't have the money, we borrow it.

I used to think that the only way to escape the "keeping up with the Jones'" lifestyle is to retreat to a convent or a commune.

I remember a pastor friend of mine telling us about a Mennonite friend of his. The area of the Shenandoah Valley in Virginia where we lived had a large number of Mennonites. Mennonites are pacifists and strive to be simple, or *plain*, in all aspects of their lives. The men and women wear very simple clothing and don't use modern technology. The Mennonites' vows of simplicity are meant to keep them from the temptations of the world and the competition of consumerism. And on Sunday mornings, you would see rows of horse and buggies full of Mennonite families going to church. From a distance all the buggies are exactly the same: black.

Our pastor told me about a conversation he had with his Mennonite friend. The pastor was commenting about the materialism he sees in society and how nice it must be for the Mennonites who don't face rampant materialism. His Mennonite friend said that even among the Mennonites there is competition in wanting to keep up. He said if you look closely, some of the buggies have silver studs lining the doors, which serve no practical purpose. They only serve to adorn the buggy. And then a week or two later you'll notice another family's buggy with similar type studs.

The competition of consumerism is in our hearts, but is manifested in different degrees. I will say that it is probably easier for the Mennonites to avoid the trappings of consumerism, but the fact is that until our hearts change, no amount of changing circumstances will bring the freedom we need.

I'm fascinated by Karl Rabeder, but not because he had the revelation about stuff not leading to happiness. That's interesting. But what is fascinating is that Mr. Rabeder sold the furnishings and accessories business that made his fortune, as well as his alpine villa, his farmhouse, his gliders, his Audi, and everything else he owned. Everything.

"My idea is to have nothing left. Absolutely nothing," he told *The Daily Telegraph*. "Money is counterproductive—it prevents happiness to come."

What did he do? He moved to a small wooden hut in the mountains. The entire proceeds went to charities he set up in Central and Latin America, but he does not even take a salary from these.

Is this nuts? Did he lose his mind? Listen for the motive: "More and more I heard the words: 'Stop what you are doing now—all this luxury and consumerism—and start your real life,'" he said. "I had the feeling I was working as a slave for things that I did not wish for or need. I have the feeling that there are lot of people doing the same thing."

Even though I don't have an alpine villa, I had to ask myself if I was working like a slave for things that I truly didn't want or need. Is it really living when I am striving for success, even if it's just for a little success?

The things we do matter, they have consequences. Of course, overt greed and spending exorbitant amounts on ourselves to live in luxury is plainly wrong. But our motives matter. Just look at Jesus' teaching in the Sermon on the Mount. He shocked his listeners with the fact that the desires of your heart are equally important as the actions of your body. Looking at a woman lustfully is equal to committing adultery. Being angry with your brother is equal to murdering him. And when Jesus said where your personal treasure is your heart will be also, he was speaking on the same level. He was simply stating a fact that if your actions indicate that your focus is on amassing money and possessions, big or small, then your heart is set on money and the things money can buy, and you will have no eternal value in your eternal account.

But if your actions indicate that your focus is on amassing . . .

- a wealth of love given to other people,
- joy in the life God has given you, whatever that may be,
- peace because you are not worried about this life because God is your Father,
- patience, kindness, and gentleness, because God is patient, kind, and gentle with you even though you don't deserve it,
- faithfulness to God and to others because without God being unwavering in sticking with you, you would be lost,
- goodness because Jesus is good and you want to be like Him,
- and self-control because the Holy Spirit is helping you overcome the desires of the sinful nature that still hangs on you like a dead body

. . . then that wealth is credited to you in your eternal account. It will never go away, never get stolen, never rust or burn, and you don't need insurance. God will keep it and treasure it forever.

I thought about when the rich young ruler approached Jesus and asked what he must do to inherit eternal life. Jesus told him he should sell all his possessions and give the money to the poor. But there was a second part. Jesus continued by saying, "then come and follow me." Jesus knew that this man's heart was set on amassing wealth in this world. If his heart was truly set on amassing spiritual wealth, then his actions would follow and he would be more than willing to get rid of the worldly wealth that held onto his heart before. And then he would go and follow Jesus and learn how to build wealth in the Kingdom of God.

Sadly, the rich young man walked away from Jesus. He couldn't give up his drive for success and the trappings of it.

Again, the temptation is to say that I am not like the rich young guy. I'm only middle-class and only "rule" 3 people at work who sit in cubicles. But if our heart is set on amassing success in this world, in whatever form, then we are no different. I was no different. The first question to ask is where is my heart? That is a hard question, because who can know the heart of man, even our own? I wasn't sure while climbing the ladder of success. I had to first ask God to strip me of self-deception and give me eyes to see myself as He sees me. I made myself look at each of my actions in my daily, weekly, and monthly life and ask this question:

Is this activity directed at achieving success in the world or success in the Kingdom of God?

If we take inventory of all the activities and their true purpose, then we'll find the answer to where our heart is. Maybe we'll arrive at the same conclusion as Mr. Rabeder did and take decisive action to remove those things that cloud our vision of the Kingdom of God. And then we may learn to kill the desires to fulfill our ambitions, and to follow Jesus everyday.

I had the attitude of the rich young ruler, sitting on my porch swing with my wife, until I looked around and said, "It's only a house." I had taken inventory of my life and realized that my actions to date had indicated a self-reliance that kept me from believing that I needed God and a pervasive desire for success in my career that did nothing to move me to greater love, joy, peace, patience, etc.

Was my life a loss up to that point? Was there evidence of God's work in my life and through my life? There was definitely fruit in my life and success in the Kingdom. I had seen coworkers start to want to know more about Jesus, and some wanted to know him personally, through God using me in their lives, and Jaye and I saw the Lord use us in our church. Any bystander's opinion of me would have been one of "balance." In fact, many people commented to me over the years that I seemed to have my priorities straight.

For a long time I carried around my personal "mission statement" which was like a neatly crafted synopsis of my order of priorities, carefully balancing my spiritual life, and my life in this world. Based on the world's standards, my priorities were straight and balanced.

But based on what the Bible, and specifically Jesus, had to say about my heart and my life, I needed a radical change to put myself in a position of utter dependence on God. Because only then could I be free of striving for success in the world.

But at that moment, on the porch swing, thank God, I gave up wanting the nice house and the comfortable career and was willing and able to sell the house, quit my job, and trust God for everything. And we felt a clear call from God to sell and leave, to start completely trusting Him. I was able to trust that God would provide a way for us to sell our house, move to a state we had never lived in, start a business I had never done as the means of providing for my family, get health insurance apart from the corporate plan we had survived on for 10 years (a critical necessity for my family), and get a mortgage to buy a house even though I didn't have a regular job.

We began the process of sharing the news with our extended family and friends. I know that my parents, with whom we spent a considerable amount of time, were sad. My mother had given so much of herself to help us when Jaye was pregnant and sick, and then after the twins were born. And my sisters felt the sting of our decision to move away from them. But I don't think any of them were surprised necessarily. They had seen my unconventional decisions in the forks in the road of life before and they knew I had changed through the experience with Jaye and the twins. Again it was my peers, especially the ones who didn't know me or my heart, who thought I was completely nuts. But we were going for it anyway.

So we put a for-sale by owner sign in the yard and I started trusting God.

NINE
FARMING

I've never been an extreme-sports guy, and haven't ever felt an inkling of desire to climb Mt. Everest. Skiing a black diamond on a puny eastern mountain is the most extreme I'll take any sport. I think I understand why people do climb Everest though, or why they bungee-jump or parachute off cliffs. It's the thrill of facing fear and jumping. It's doing something that is so far out of a normal, daily routine that it invigorates and inspires.

When we first arrived in Florida, and moved into our house, I took a step back and surveyed what I had done. I had some money saved, but not enough to live on for a year. Carter was 4 and the twins were barely walking. I wasn't sure about health care for my family. How was this all going to fly? God gave me the vision and faith to make the decision, but now we were committed and the details of making money in a business that I had never even remotely experienced began to weigh on my brain, and my faith. The experience must be like when the BASE jumper jumps off the cliff for the first time.

I thought again of the farmers on the frontier, and I felt a certain camaraderie with them. There are no more frontiers, but I was on a frontier in my world. And instead of farming fields of crops, I was farming houses, trying to invest my time, money, and effort in bringing in a harvest.

Little by little, and day by day, God provided ways to make money to pay our bills. I had a business partner, Matthias, who knew about as much as I did about houses. I knew how to paint houses from my experience with my father growing up in New York, but beyond that we had very little knowledge of how to fix anything. We both struggled with waiting for God to provide.

One day, I got a call from a lady who said she wanted to sell her house and wanted us to come look at it. I asked about the condition of the house, and she said it needed a lot of work, which made me immediately cringe. But then she told me the price she wanted, which was low enough that it was worth a look. It had rotten siding, a leaking roof, a nasty kitchen, a leaking bathtub, etc. She wasn't kidding about a lot of work.

Matthias and I talked it over and decided that this was a great opportunity to learn "on the job" by doing the renovations ourselves, saving money on the labor costs, and then selling it for a decent profit. So we bought the house, loaded up the 10 tools we had between us and started plugging away to redeem the little yellow house.

One day, I was there by myself trying to take a stab at the leaky bathtub. I started taking apart the valve to find the problem, having really no idea what I was looking for. I kept taking things apart thinking I would find water dripping where it shouldn't be dripping, and remove and replace whatever "thingy" needed replacing.

Having experience in repairing houses is important, but sometimes a little common sense is more important. I got down to the main part of the valve and saw where the drip was coming from. But I had to take the valve cartridge out get to it. So I grabbed my pliers and pulled. It was tight, so I planted my feet firmly on the tub and yanked. Out it came, along with a deluge of spraying water. I didn't think of turning the water main off before taking a major plumbing fixture apart.

It made me think of the time in college that I got 4 traffic tickets at once, and in court the judge asked me what I was studying. After I told him, he said I needed to "go back and take a course in common sense."

After the house dried out, we finished it, put it on the market, and quickly sold it. Renovating houses to flip wasn't part of our game plan, but it was God showing us that He provides what we need when we need it. The experience gave us the confidence to continue rehabbing houses and learning more with each deal. It was another little step in building my faith.

Building my faith; that's exactly what God was doing, and I was willing, but not always feeling able. Those first few years, God provided over and over again. Worry still crept in, wanting to choke me, but God kept reminding me that He is my Father and He doesn't want me to worry and act like He isn't there. My desire for security was still palpable, still tempting my heart to find ways to prop up my self-supports. Worry about the future and the lingering desire for security caused me to make a lot of bad decisions as I was still learning to trust and not rush to a decision, to pray and wait for an answer even though it is hard to maintain faith when you don't know where your income will come from next. But throughout, without fail, God provided over and over again, what we needed, when we needed it. It doesn't mean there weren't losses, there were. But God provided. Even when there was still a part of me that wanted wealth and the easy life of passive income.

Despite my mixed motivations, I was learning in deeper, more abiding ways, that God is my Father and has purpose for my life, and that with Him there are no coincidences. I saw His hand in more and more details of my life. I was learning that my Father desires my trust in Him to provide for our needs of life, but also to trust Him for all the events of life. I was learning that it is one thing to trust Him for money, food, clothing, and shelter. It is another to trust Him for events that are painful and don't make sense.

Jeff and Cami built a house right next door to us so we were living in real community, our small group at our church was great, and we were growing together and learning to love. Jeff was the youth pastor at our church, and he was really thriving in his ministry. The senior pastor, the one who hired Jeff, was ready to retire after 25 years, which brought certain uncertainty to our congregation. The people in charge of finding a new pastor contacted the pastor of our church in Virginia, the one who married us, who happened to be looking for a new call. After a long interview process, they offered him the position, and he accepted.

I could not believe it. There we were, living next door to our great friends learning about community, in a fabulous small group of young couples in church, watching God work in our lives in real ways, and our favorite pastor was coming to our church. I told people that I must be God's favorite. How could it get better?

When our old Virginia pastor became our church's new pastor, there was, as there usually is, a honeymoon phase where everyone loved each other and all was well. When that phase ended, there was a painful but stark reality emerging that Jeff and the new pastor were very different people, with very different philosophies on how church is done. I chose not to believe it at first, but the reality became too vivid that I couldn't avoid it any longer. After some time, the differences between the pastor and Jeff were too strong to endure, and Jeff would have to leave.

I went from joking about being God's favorite, to now being in another very difficult test of faith, wondering out loud what God could possibly be doing. I believed that God had clearly called us there, and we obeyed, putting our faith in Him. But why would He bring this radical change in our lives, put us in an amazing community, only to break it all up? I knew God had a reason, I had learned that much. But I couldn't, for the life of me, understand.

As we all talked and prayed through this terrible and trying time, we came to the possibility that God was calling us to plant a new church, to start a new community. Our small group was made up mostly of people who live around us, and we came to think that a new church must be God's plan. Why else would He do this? Jeff would be the pastor, and we would form a new congregation.

There had always been talk at church to plant in the area we lived anyway. It made sense. Jeff was warm to the idea, but I could tell he was reluctant, never really feeling completely comfortable with being a church planter. But we pressed on with the planning, feeling this had to be God's plan.

In the middle of the planning process, I went on a short-term trip to Monterrey, Mexico with our church, as I had done many times before. I became fluent in Spanish as a teenager, when my parents sent me to Mexico for a summer to live with their good Mexican friends. The passion to learn was in my heart from an early age, and I was the only one of my parents' four kids to learn. Now seeing that God works intentionally in His children's lives, I wondered what His purpose was to lead me to learn Spanish. I briefly thought of being a missionary, but with Jaye's health concerns that would be impossible. Our church's relationship with ministries in Monterrey gave me an outlet to serve in small ways a couple of times a year at least.

I went on the trip, translating and helping in any other way I could, as I did on every other trip to Monterrey. This time, however, there was a guy named Tim who came along. Tim is a 6'8" giant of a man, who everyone calls "Timo." I think when you are that tall and strong, people have to put an "O" at the end of your name. Timo is the funniest person I have ever met, and most people who know him think so, except for the people who don't think Christians should laugh that much. He also happens to be an incredibly godly man who loves Jesus with a passion and wants others to see Him too. Timo and I hit it off, and we spent a lot of time together that weekend, mostly talking about our new church plant idea.

At the end of our trip, we were sitting in the airport in Monterrey, Mexico, waiting to board our flight. We were sitting around a table sipping coffee with a few other people, and Timo turned to me, grabbed my chair, and pulled it towards his.

For a second I wasn't laughing; I was afraid of his giant hands. Timo leaned over and said, "I've never met anyone like you."

"Uh, what do you mean?"

"I've been watching you this weekend with the Mexican people. You speak like one of them, you fit right into their culture, you even eat tortillas the right way. They love you."

He went on, "Where I live, there a ton of Hispanic men working all around our church. I want to love them, to share Jesus with them, but I can't. I can't communicate with them, I don't know their culture, and I'm too big; I'd scare them off. But you can. You need to be in a ministry to Hispanic people."

And just like that my life was again changed.

On a human level you could look at all of these circumstances and conversations that converge on one another as mere coincidences, accidental happenings as I walked down life's road. This was no coincidence; I stopped believing in coincidences. He was right, and I knew that this was God telling me, calling me again. It was a peace I felt inside even though it made little sense, given that the rational explanation of God's plan for our community was to plant a church.

I came home, and as Jaye and I sat down to talk about the trip, I began to tell her about Timo, and all about his little conversation with me in the airport. I told Jaye that I felt God was calling me to get involved in ministering to Hispanic people, and that He was using the situation between Jeff and the senior pastor to make me see it. I gave her space for God to speak to her, but it took very little time for Jaye to see it and hear God's call as well.

Jeff and Cami were scheduled to go to a center to be assessed on whether or not they are suitable church planters, while they were thinking that church planting was God's answer to the "why" of this painful situation. Around the same time of my Monterrey trip, Jeff got a call from a church in Atlanta about their search for a new youth pastor. This is the kind of church Jeff was being trained for all of his adult life, but seemed way too good to be true.

I started investigating Hispanic ministries that Jaye and I could get plugged into. We didn't feel that God was telling us to start something new, but rather to come alongside and be a support to an existing ministry. I contacted the person in charge of Hispanic ministry in our denomination and asked him if there were any opportunities to help in my area in Florida. He said that there weren't any projects in my area, and then asked if we were willing to move. I told him that yes, we were willing, because we felt this was God's call and He would provide. He felt the best thing to do is to spend a weekend together talking and praying about it together. He told me that the greatest needs in our denomination were in Houston, Texas, Atlanta, and Harrisonburg, the town in Virginia where our college, James Madison University, sits; bizarre, given our college ties to Harrisonburg and Jeff's interview with the Atlanta church.

While we were planning the trip to meet up with the Hispanic Ministry Director in Atlanta, Jeff went through the interview process with the big Atlanta church, and was given the position. So we planned our trip to look for God's will again.

Jaye and I wanted to be very careful about discerning God's will in this, because we didn't want our will to be done, but His. It meant we would be leaving our other great friends Lindsay and Matthias, who was my business partner, behind. We had great community with them as well. "Matindsay" we called them, lived a few blocks away from us, and Matthias and I spent every day working together for 4 years, trying to make a living while learning how to be entrepreneurs. This couldn't be a decision made lightly because we knew this move would be very painful for us all. Before the trip, and on our way, we prayed constantly about it, asking God to show us what to do and to give us wisdom. We met with Hispanic Director guy, prayed a lot, and asked him to tell us what he thought. He asked us a lot of questions, and we prayed some more.

It is patently difficult to discern God's will in every situation. There are things that are clearly spelled out in the Bible, with lines that we don't cross. But God's will in so many of the decisions of life aren't easily discernible. When we see that God is truly sovereign and does work *all* things together for the good of those who love Him, then we by faith believe that there are no coincidences, that He speaks to us in still, small voices sometimes, in big 6'8" voices others, and through opened and closed doors.

There were so many ways we felt God calling us to Atlanta that weekend: meeting Alejandro and Ludi, pastor of the new bilingual church plant in the Atlanta area, and finding that our vision and philosophies match up. Getting a vision for the ways God might use us to help get the church off the ground. God was calling us to a church plant after all, just not the one we thought. And I believe that God takes joy in the community we share with our good friends, and He didn't want that to end just yet.

So we came back and began preparing for the move, which we would wait a year to do, also believing that was God's desire for us to not leave abruptly. We talked to Jeff and Cami, and we all decided that if God would open the door that we would try to live next door to each other again. But about 10 different variables would have to come together, in order, at the right time, for it to work. We again found ourselves believing that God would intervene and make it clear that it was His hand.

Jeff and Cami were going to move a full year before us. They needed to sell their house in Florida, and once they sold their house they needed to be able to buy and move into their new house. We thought we could build houses next door to one another, but Jeff found out quickly that there were no new houses being built anywhere near our target area. We were forced into looking for 2 existing homes.

Our real estate agents, Scott and Rachel, were given the formidable and uneasy task of finding a solution to our dilemma. Scott got major-league proactive and drove to the houses for sale that Jeff and Cami were interested in and knocked on the neighbor's doors to ask if they were thinking about selling any time in the next year. Scott then told us about one neighbor of a vacant house for sale that he approached. Scott rattled off the scenario for the 100th time, and the owner said, "That's funny. My wife and I have been praying about selling our house, and we decided that we didn't want to go through the hassles of listings and showings, but if God brings us a buyer, then we would sell."

There were several things that had to happen for this little miracle of finding 2 houses next door to each other again to work out. Affordable and reasonable prices for both houses, financing, the timing of us not being able to close on the house for another 8 months. And it all came together as if it were planned from the start.

So there it was. I wasn't surprised, but rather I was excited to tell again of God's hand in our lives, to encourage people that He is real, that He really wants us to trust Him, to seek first His Kingdom, and all these other things will be added.

I now had eight months to pray, and ask God to show me how I would again move to a new city, and provide for my family. The initial excitement of the decision faded and again the reality sunk in, and worry again perked up in my little, fickle heart. Not like before, but it still was there, as I pondered the future with giant question marks.

Five months before the move, Jeff and I decided to meet up at a state campground to spend a couple of days in silent prayer and thought. I needed the time to get away and really seek God. To try to hear Him, to ask Him to give me direction about business, and how to approach the task of providing. Jeff and I would wake up, have breakfast, and then go silent for the rest of the day so we could each focus on hearing from God. The second day I decided to load up my Bible and notepad and take a long walk. I wandered around the lake in the park and headed up a sparsely traveled road. Halfway up a hill, I took a detour into the woods to find a quiet place to sit. About 200 meters into the woods, I came across a pond settled in the bottom of a ravine, and an old tree stand that I could perch on for a while.

I sat there in silence for a long time, just taking it all in, trying to get quiet in my heart. Then I looked across the pond, and there was an egret, a beautiful white bird, also perched on a tree stump. I thought I would watch him for a while. I watched as he took off, dove into the water, and flew back to his perch. He did this over and over again. It was beautiful. As I absorbed this tiny picture of God's order of things, I opened my Bible to Matthew 6 and read Jesus' words to His disciples, "Do not worry about your life; what you will eat or drink; or about your body, what you will wear. Is not life more important than food, and the body more important than clothes? Look at the birds of the air; they do not sow or reap or store away in barns, and yet your heavenly Father feeds them. Are you not much more valuable than they?" The egret was fishing. God was literally feeding that bird in front of my eyes. That egret didn't have a bank account, real estate, or even a little hole to store his excess fish. And he wasn't worried a bit about it.

It occurred to me that God had literally led me to this spot to see this egret fishing. He communicated to me that He loves me, that He is my Father, that He wants me again to trust Him, in everything, for everything. He reminded me that in seeking first His Kingdom and His righteousness, the fruit of the Spirit, I would be used for His purposes for His greatest glory. And He will take care of the rest. I walked away with the clear, strong conviction of His love and peace and didn't worry about how He would provide. I knew I was like a farmer, doing the daily task of preparing soil, planting seed, pulling weeds, watering, and trusting God to grow the plant and bring fruit.

Five months later we made the move, and we started helping Alejandro and Ludi get the new church off the ground. I purchased my first house to flip, and had it ready to sell. Money was very tight as I was starting over in a new city. I found myself on my knees at 3am, not worried that God wouldn't provide like earlier in my life, but asking Him if I was in His will, doing what He wanted me to do, and asking for Him to show me. And the very next day He brought a buyer for the house, showing me to keep on plugging away, that I was doing what He wanted. Once again, God had mercy on my fickle faith and showed me the way.

I've been "farming" for 8 years now. There have been so many things I have tried to see if they would work in providing an income; so many seeds I've planted and watered and nourished to see if they would grow. Not every seed I've planted has grown successfully. In fact, most haven't, like the Spanish radio show on finances, or the insurance license I got but never used.

I believe God wants me to plant seeds, water them for a while to see if they grow, and to believe Him through it all, not worrying about tomorrow.

I fell into getting my general contractor's license by mistake when another real estate investor convinced me that I would be sued for renovating houses without it.

Friends began asking me if I knew people who could fix roofs, or install carpet, or fix their air conditioning. "Why yes," I began saying. And so began a little ancillary source of income. I've never advertised, but God has brought many friends of friends of friends to my cell phone needing new roofs, bathrooms, kitchens, decks, you name it. And it's all very messy and good for my character.

Just recently we did a remodel job for a young couple, transforming their 1950 tiny kitchen and bathroom into a modern space. I was standing there covered in drywall dust talking to the husband, thinking how far I had come from the big office building and the Polo suit and tie. He asked me how I got into contractor work. Oh, what a question. I knew he wasn't looking for an answer the length of the first 70 pages of this book.

So I told him I wanted to live for what mattered, so I decided to leave the corporate life. He asked what I did before, and I told him. He stared at me for an awkward 20 seconds, not knowing how to respond, probably thinking, "Did he go to jail or something?"

I've had several of those moments, and the most interesting ones are with people in the church who are on the success ladder. Because not only are they confused about me, I'm confused about them that they are confused about me. To me it seems so obvious that we should forsake success for Jesus' sake and the sake of our wives, or husbands, our kids, our friends, our communities. But it isn't obvious. It wasn't obvious to me until God grabbed me, shook me violently, and changed me.

This life of radical faith probably looks foolish to most. But I long to see God really intervening in my life and the lives of people around me, so that it can't be said that I am playing a religious game and living a charade.

This life of trusting my Father has taught me so much, and He has changed me so much. I no longer have these compartmentalized little "lives" that I keep balanced on a ledger. I'm on a path now to live all of my life under one unified purpose; a quest to find His will, live His will, to live as Jesus taught. But I am so far from it. I only know that I am closer now than I was 8 years ago. It's impossible to be completely and perfectly focused on living for Jesus and His purposes, but I believe that we can be set in the right direction, or we can be set in the wrong direction. Once God set me in the right direction He began to make me think deeply about the things that matter to Him, and thus the things that ultimately matter. And I discovered that His list isn't that long.

They are simple concepts, but the hardest to do well. Loving my wife, my children, and my community. Loving God. As He caused me to think about these aspects of life that truly matter, I looked back on each of them to see how He was there at each joyful moment, and painful one, teaching me and changing me and pointing me in the right direction once again. Reflecting on what He taught me about marriage, family, and community I see from my story how hard it is to be faithful to live out His plan and purpose.

History is the greatest teacher. And when I forget about ultimate and eternal issues and get caught up in the trivial and mundane, I think about the deeper story of my marriage, the grace of God in how each of my children came about, and the joy and sanctification that comes in real community. When I forget about what I'm really here for I remember, and it grounds me again.

TEN
SOAP

I acknowledge that not everyone is wired the same way. Some are gifted with the ability to truly live the single, celibate life, and not turn into very strange people. For the rest of us, marriage is one of our greatest aspirations. To be committed to one another in a sacred manner by making vows before God and man, till death do us part, is a thrilling and awesome endeavor. The vows we take vary. Some are taken from Scripture, some are written by our own hands. In every case, we vow to be committed to each other.

Jaye and I knew early on in our relationship in college that we were meant for each other. It's funny, but we never used the "M" word with each other. It wasn't as if we talked about it occasionally, or even once. We never used the word *marriage* in conversation with each other until I proposed. It was like a phobia that if the word were mentioned it would spoil the surprise. We just knew that God had set us up and it was His doing.

We got married 2 months after we graduated from JMU, the first of any of our friends. Being the first made weddings a new, really cool thing for all of our college buddies. No one was worn out yet by the wave of weddings that happen the few years after college. And my father-in-law throws an amazing party. Needless to say, the wedding was a complete blast.

Neither Jaye nor I had been to any weddings, except maybe as kids. We had no idea that you can ask your musically talented friends to come and play a cool acoustic Bread or Dan Fogelberg song. The wedding coordinator lady and the resident organist must have deep down loved us because ours had to be the easiest wedding they did all year, maybe in 10 years. It must have been the fastest wedding of any we have been to since. I think the ceremony lasted 19 minutes, from "Here Comes the Bride" to "Wedding March", *literally*.

The greatest moment was when I was waiting at the altar. There was a pause after the organist finished the prelude. He started playing the high-pitched intro to "Here Comes the Bride" and my heart started to pound. I looked down the isle at the closed doors that had glass windows in each shaped in the form of a cross. Through the cross I saw Jaye. The doors swung open and they entered the sanctuary. I had heard the word *radiant* before but never knew what it really meant. Sure, I knew the written definition, but I didn't *know* the word. It was a word I experienced at that moment.

Jaye was *radiant*.

In a completely spontaneous outburst I said, "Oh *wow*." The music didn't matter, or the candles, or the flowers. There was my beautiful bride walking towards me to become mine, and I hers.

A few years later our pastor who married us was giving a sermon on Ephesians 5.

Husbands, love your wives, just as Christ loved the church and gave himself up for her to make her holy, cleansing her by the washing with water through the word, and to present her to himself as a radiant church, without stain or wrinkle or any other blemish, but holy and blameless. In this same way, husbands ought to love their wives as their own bodies. He who loves his wife loves himself.

He wanted to give us a picture of how Jesus feels about us, His Bride, the Church. He wanted to show us that Jesus doesn't come to us under obligation. Christ comes to us running. He is filled with heart-felt affection for His Bride. Then our pastor told the story of standing next to me at our wedding and observing how I reacted when I saw Jaye coming down the isle.

"That is how Christ feels about you," he said. "His Church."

Knowing how passionately and sacrificially Jesus loves us is really intimidating when I think that I am called to love Jaye the same way. How we love our wives is a picture of how we love God. There was a moment, a dark and sad moment, when God revealed my heart and and gave me a glimpse of how my love of money was competing with my love for Jaye, and ultimately my love for God.

• • •

When I was dating Jaye in college, and then engaged at the end of college, I had a vague knowledge of the term "honeymoon phase." I heard the term used in different contexts, but if my knowledge of the term was vague, my understanding of it was tiny. I knew the basic purpose of the term, but I hadn't experienced what it really meant so I couldn't fully understand it. Well after I got married and experienced marriage for a while, the term sunk in and now I have a robust understanding of the phrase.

I think I was probably really nice and courteous when we first got married, tempering my speech with sweetness and romance. But that goes away when you realize how hard it is to keep it up all the time when you really feel like being your natural self, which in my case is a jerk.

The first year after we moved to Charlotte, I won a sales trip to St. Thomas in the U.S. Virgin Islands. This was an all-expense paid, mack-daddy, week-long resort vacation, with built-in all-day excursions on sail boats for snorkeling at a secluded coral reef, jet-ski lessons, and free shuttle trips to historic downtown Charlotte Amalie and its shopping district. The first 2 excursion options sounded great to both of us. The third sounded great to Jaye.

We did the sailboat thing and made a great time of it. Then it came time to do the tour of the downtown shopping district. I think I would rather sit in a hot prison cell with 4 smelly men than walk through a shopping district, historic or not. But it is what Jaye wanted to do. So I signed up for it.

We got on the shuttle bus and trekked across the island to the downtown area of Charlotte Amalie, St. Thomas. The moment we stepped off the bus we were deluged with people offering us free gifts, like airplane tickets, if we just spent 60 minutes looking at their time-share property.

Now, I could go shopping if I could get some significant something for free out of it, so things were looking up. Jaye looked at me and said, "Kyle, I really want to see downtown."

"I know but this won't take long. *Free* airline tickets . . ." I replied in an authoritatively convincing manner. Jaye looked disappointed and suspicious, but come-on, we're talking about *free airline tickets.*

We went with the slick salesman while everyone else on the tour shuffled off into the interesting downtown experience. They were going to lose money; I was going to come out ahead.

We climbed a hill to this area that was lined with apartment-like buildings and cottages. The slickster took us into one of the buildings to show off their *amazing* architecture, as if block buildings with stucco look any different in Charlotte Amalie than in Charlotte, NC.

Jaye glanced over and gave me a distinct "can we please leave now?" kind of look.

We proceeded to another building, then another. I was ready to collect my tickets and go, but they wanted me to hear how great it would be for my life to own a timeshare vacation. I didn't want a time-share, I wanted the plane tickets. I told them that as Jaye squeezed my hand. Then we had to sit down at a table until the "manager" came. This guy was *Mr.* Slickster and he began to pour it on, all the while Jaye is driving her heal into my foot under the table to let me know she is not happy and wants to get out of there so we can see downtown before the shuttle bus comes to pick us up.

I couldn't shake this guy. I thought I was Mr. Tough Guy and could get out of here quickly, but this guy was above my game. We spent 90 minutes listening to this garbage until I finally convinced them I wasn't buying. They gave me my airline ticket "vouchers" and we left.

Jaye looked at her watch and we had 10 minutes left. 10 minutes of the allotted time to experience Old St. Thomas. It wasn't even enough time to walk there, let alone get back.

When I first met Jaye, all of her high school friends at JMU told me how pure she was, how they had never heard her swear. Ever. And that held true all the time I knew her. Up until then.

We found our way to a park bench near the shuttle bus pick up spot. I sat on one side and Jaye found the farthest corner from me she could nestle into. Then it came out.

"How could you do that?! You knew I wanted to see downtown. Why didn't you get us out of there?"

"I . . . I thought.."

"It's the only thing I wanted to do! I can't believe you!"

"Well, I . . ."

"I AM SO #$*@ING MAD AT YOU!!" as she folded her arms in absolute disgust and turned away from me, face completely red with righteous anger.

I sat in cold silence, in complete and total shock. I had succeeded in bringing just wrath out of Jaye, this angel on earth, and it spewed all over the place. We were given the all-expense paid, amazing vacation, and I robbed my wife of the one simple *free* thing she wanted to do. The thing is, Jaye isn't a shopper at all. In fact, she's the least materialistic person I know. She just wanted to see this old Caribbean town. And I stole that from her, all because I didn't want to do it and I thought I could get something out of it.

Not only was I selfish, I was a complete cheapskate when I should be lavishing generosity on my wife, *especially* knowing I hadn't spent a dime on this trip.

Needless to say, the honeymoon phase was over. And we never used the airline ticket "vouchers" (the small print stinks).

That was a pivotal moment in my life and in our marriage. Not that I did an about face and shunned all my selfishness from there on out. It was more like a wake-up call and flash of awareness about my role as a husband.

• • •

As a follower of Jesus, I have a lot of calls on my life. The greatest call which is to love God and love people, and under that umbrella is the call to be a servant, to reach out to those who don't know Jesus, etc.

But this call, "Husbands love your wives as Christ loves the church" seemed to be the highest for me in terms of human relationships. I began to see that it wasn't enough for me to take care of Jaye's physical and emotional needs.

I am pretty aware of Jaye's physical needs because of her cystic fibrosis and diabetes. It's an ever-present reality that we need to be diligent in taking care of her body.

What I fall short in is giving myself up for her. God was calling me to die to myself, my selfishness, and wash her with the word and work to present her to God as spiritually radiant. This is a heavy task.

My affection for her has always been powerful. But I found my affection for myself to be pretty high too. It still is, unfortunately. After I began really understanding this call me for as a husband, I began seeing how much I do on a daily basis to make sure that I am spiritually grounded, comfortable, and happy.

But how do I bathe Jaye in the word of God? Do I pray for her, and encourage her in her walk with God? Do I really care for her in practical ways every day like I care for myself? Or do I just cause her to cuss?

As I think about wanting to be a good and faithful servant of my King in the Kingdom, His call for me to love Jaye as Christ loves the Church is on top of the list of principles. I say that knowing how far I fall short. I am so glad God gave her to me because she is the closest human embodiment of 1 Corinthians 13, the "love chapter," that I have ever known. And without her patience with me in struggling to love her well I would surely and permanently fail.

I wonder sometimes if I would be different if Jaye didn't have cystic fibrosis. I don't know. I might not be as aware of her needs or the preciousness of every day God gives us. But I know that He brought us together and has used her health concerns to focus my heart on what is important. And I am incredibly grateful for that.

God is also teaching me to trust Him for Jaye, that her health is in His hands. My most fervent prayer the first 10 years of my Christian life was that God would heal Jaye, which I still believe He can do. But I don't pray that prayer much anymore. Not that I don't want it, or don't believe He can, but I just believe that He is sovereign over her life and health, and He has a plan, which is perfect.

In that peace I can learn to love her more deeply and practically, not out of fear, but out of love for God.

The definition of real success in my life includes loving Jaye the way Jesus loves us. Jesus is scrubbing me down every day, washing off all that isn't like Him. Every time I go backwards and get soiled digging in the garbage can to find satisfaction instead of finding satisfaction in Him, Jesus brings me back and cleans me up and invites me again to the beautiful table He prepared for me, to taste and see that He is good.

ELEVEN
ARROWS

When I became a Christian in college I read a lot about a particular man who helped countless others come to know the love of God and find forgiveness. This guy was a hero to me. He was a true evangelist. He wouldn't go to sleep at night if he hadn't shared with someone that God offers forgiveness if we only trust in the life, death, and resurrection of Christ. I wanted that passion. It was 3 years later that I found myself talking with the first son of that man. I wanted to soak up all I could from the son of my hero, and so I asked him what it was like to be his son. He looked at me in the eyes and said, "I hated him."

The man I was talking to was not a hardened atheist, anti-Jesus type. That would make the hate understandable to me. He loved Jesus. He just hated his father for the first 60 years of his life. He then went on to explain that his father was never there, and spent all of his time with other people and not his family. He was doing great things by teaching many, many people about the Kingdom, but he sacrificed his wife and children in the process. God clearly used this man, and my new, real life following Jesus was an indirect result of this man's ministry.

The conversation really made me question a lot of things. Questions like: If a man or woman leads many people to faith in Jesus and therefore many people now have eternal life because God used that person, but yet he or she doesn't really invest in their family, is that being a good and faithful servant, or a successful Christian? If someone is a full-time

Christian worker and is devoted to serving people, but doesn't really serve his wife and kids, is that a picture of success in God's eyes?

Maybe that man read Mark 10:28-30 and made a conscious decision that it was necessary for the sake of expanding God's kingdom to leave his family behind.

"Peter said to him, 'We have left everything to follow you!'

'I tell you the truth,' Jesus replied, 'no one who has left home or brothers or sisters or mother or father or children or fields for me and the gospel will fail to receive a hundred times as much in this present age (homes, brothers, sisters, mothers, children and fields—and with them, persecutions) and in the age to come, eternal life.'"

Maybe he thought that for the sake of the thousands, and maybe millions, that God would save through his work that it was necessary to sacrifice good relationships with his family. There seems to be a tension between that perspective and "Husbands love your wives as Christ loved the Church" and with, "Fathers, do not exasperate your children. Instead, bring them up in the training and instruction of the Lord."

I have over the years struggled with these questions in my desire to be a good and faithful servant, but I can't. Maybe it's a specific calling for certain people. As my heart sunk when I heard that man say that he hated his father for 60 years, including long after his father died, I knew that it wasn't my calling to leave my family behind. In fact, that experience made me double down in my desire to be a godly husband and eventual father. I decided that if my kids hate me when they are older because I love God, then so be it. But if they hate me because I didn't love them, then, according to what I believe God is calling me to, I am the worst kind of man.

When I had just begun in the training program with the bank, I was working in a local branch as part of my training. There was a little 4'10" lady from Peru who worked as a teller. We hit it off because she loved that I was a gringo who spoke Spanish like a Mexican. She and her husband didn't make much money and they had 4 kids. One day she and I were talking about my desire to be a father, but I felt I wasn't ready financially and emotionally to be a good father.

She looked up and with a simple, peaceful smile said, "Children are a blessing. God will give you what you need. Don't worry." Her faith was strong, and I envied that.

About a year after we got married, Jaye and I decided to have children. It was our decision. *Our* decision. It wasn't God's decision.

We tried and tried, but no pregnancy. For some reason, we just couldn't get pregnant. We shared our problem with our families. My family is a big, close-knit bunch full of women who don't mind sharing opinions, which we were wide open to. One such member told us that the key to solving the problem is a turkey baster. But she never explained how the technique actually works. We tried the turkey baster. No pregnancy. Maybe falling out of bed laughing your head off keeps it from working.

After over a year of trying we decided it was time to see a fertility specialist. After they did their tests, we were given a plan to start on the very basic fertility treatments: artificial insemination, where they essentially take my little troopers and with a long tube place them at *just* the right spot to find Jaye's waiting Cadbury's.

We were scheduled for our first appointment and I told Jaye I wasn't doing this alone. We arrived at the hospital and meandered through the basement level hallways until we found the fertility hall. We made our way to the clinic and checked in. They could just tell we were newbies by the look of horror on my face.

A sweet, little lady who looked like my mother asked if we had done this before, at which I quipped sharply, "No," She told us to follow her to "the room."

We trotted on down the hall and came to a door that could have been mistaken for the janitor's closet. She knocked softly, and listened for a reply, heard none, and opened the door. We followed her into this room that was all of 6' x 6', had a futon style half sized couch, a TV with VCR and a bunch of cabinets. She asked if I was going to do this alone, and I said, "Nope." She then proceeded to open the cabinet doors. The first cabinet had a stack of magazines, the second a stack of videos. Then looking at us with a tender smile and pointing at the three levels of videos said, "The top shelf is X, the middle shelf is XX, and the bottom shelf is XXX. There are also magazines if you don't want to do videos, it's up to you."

"Push me into the grave, I'm going to die," I thought. It was unbelievably surreal to be taking lessons on how to effectively use porn from what could be my mother.

Well, we got through it and trotted on back down the hall in sheer awkwardness to deliver to the ladies my plastic cup full of goods in a clearly marked paper bag. And I got out of there as fast as I could.

We waited the customary three or so weeks to see if God would give us a little one, but Jaye's monthly friend came instead. No baby.

So off I was again the next month for another appointment. This time Jaye said I was on my own. Oh boy . . . I avoided Ma Bailey this time; I just grabbed my little brown bag and headed off for the futon room. Again, I ran out of there as fast as I could.

Three weeks later her period arrived again. No baby.

Every month we did the treatments. And nothing happened. They increased the dosage of medication. And still nothing. We tried and tried and tried. Before long we became buddies with the whole crew. I knew all the ladies on a first name basis and would walk in, chat a while with them, go off to the futon room, come back with my soldiers and chat a little longer before saying goodbye.

After trying for so long, Jaye and I were spent. We believed God was going to use this for good, we just didn't know how. We started considering that maybe God was calling us to adopt.

In the midst of that discussion, a friend who knew what we were going through called and said she had a contact in Pennsylvania who handled adoptions. We got in contact with that person who immediately told us that there was a girl in their town who called them wanting to give her child up for adoption who would be born in a few months. It seemed as though God was opening a door.

Within a few days we drove to Pennsylvania to meet with the adoption contact. She wanted us to meet with the girl to see if it was a fit. With a ton of anticipation, we drove to the run-down house this young girl was renting and knocked on the door. She opened the door and excitedly invited us in and started talking all about her situation.

Within 5 minutes she started referring to Jaye and I as the ones who are going to adopt the baby, as if it were a foregone conclusion. The entire conversation continued as if she had already made up her mind and we were the ones.

We drove home excited and a bit stunned. It all seemed like it was going to come together and we would adopt this new baby. God had been preparing our hearts to see the beauty of adoption, just as He adopted us.

We continued the infertility treatments and routine, month after month for well over a year. It was a major emotional roller coaster, waiting for the results, waiting on God to answer. But Jaye was at peace, a peace that is not in the realm of logical understanding, but only comes by God's power.

Eventually, she decided it was time to call it quits; no more infertility treatments. While we were waiting to hear news from Pennsylvania, Jaye reconsidered and decided to go through the infertility routine one last time, just to lay the whole thing to rest once and for all. So we contacted the hospital and made our appointment to say goodbye to the whole process.

I've found in so many different circumstances in my life that God wants me to remember that He is my Father, my Sustainer, my Provider, my Comforter, my Satisfaction, and my Peace. He uses circumstances to teach me to trust Him, and Him alone. I forget, I get worried, and I start trusting in something or someone else. But He always enters into my life in clear ways to remind me.

While we were starting to think more seriously about getting ready to adopt, Jaye asked if I wanted to meet her for lunch. We met up in a little Deli in north Charlotte. I walked in and found her sitting in the back. She was quiet, but normal. I thought that the nurses must have called and given her the bad news once again. I made small talk to distract from the inevitably painful conversation and we ordered some sandwiches.

After the food arrived Jaye looked at me with tears in her eyes, grabbed my hand across the table, and said, "I'm pregnant."

We shared tears together. Not just because years of trying had finally come to an end. And not just because we knew we would have a child of our own. But also because God gave us this child at the moment we both came to the point where we truly trusted Him in this, that His will was best for us, whatever His will is. He taught us to trust Him, not in an abstract way, but in a way that says, "Whatever you want Lord, we want." At the moment He had our hearts, He gave us our first child, a girl we named Carter.

We called our adoption contact immediately to find out any news with the young pregnant girl, feeling a bit overwhelmed with the thought of adopting and pregnancy at the same time. But we believed God was sovereign and if he wanted us to adopt this child while Jaye was pregnant, then we would adopt with complete openness and love.

We weren't told the reason, but the girl changed her mind and decided to keep the baby. She didn't even know we were pregnant.

Two years after Carter we revisited the infertility doctor, and after several treatments, along came the twins. Life for our little family has been wonderful. Jaye and I settled into a mode of parenting, trying to model God as much as possible for them. We started envisioning our kids as teenagers in just a few years, and all that entails, and that started making us feel old for the first time.

In October of 2009, for some odd reason I was talking on the phone with my sister, Erika, and she asked about birth control, if we use it. I laughed and told her that Jaye can't get pregnant on her own, so we have built-in birth control. It just can't happen.

A few weeks later, I was driving home from work and I got a call from Jaye asking me to pick up a pregnancy test. I thought it was odd but didn't think much of it because with Jaye's health her period is often late.

But, you know, women like to be sure.

I came in and dropped the test on the table, descended into my office and moved along with my day. Jaye popped in a few minutes later with the test in hand. Those two blue lines were solid and bright.

I stared at her a moment and then broke out into hysterical laughter, holding my jaw up from hitting the floor. I laughed out of complete shock for a week. In fact, I'm still laughing. I cannot believe that after 15 years of marriage, and 7 years after the twins, God gave us a baby.

The doctor gave us the due date, and Carter, after looking in her own baby book, found that the baby and Carter had exactly the same due date. Carter was born 7 days before her due date, and we told her the chances of the baby being born on the same day were very low.

But 9 months later, our baby girl was born, a little after midnight, exactly 10 years to the day after Carter was born. The same birthday.

It's as if God was telling us yet again: there are *no* coincidences. He is working out the plan of our lives with complete perfection.

We all felt it this time. Here was a picture of His grace lavished on us. So we named her the best word we could come up with: Grace. There is no better name than Grace for her to carry in our family and in her life. She will be and have a constant reminder of God's grace, how He loves us and cares for us.

He loves us so much, He reminds us in amazing and surprising ways to trust Him in everything.

I read years ago the passage in Psalm 127:

"Sons are a heritage from the Lord,
    children a reward from him.
    Like arrows in the hands of a warrior are
    sons born in one's youth.

Blessed is the man whose quiver is full of them. They will not be put to shame when they contend with their enemies in the gate."

When I think about my children, when I see their smiles and hear their constant laughter, I get a deep sense that they are a reward to me from my Father. Each one of them represents a time when God taught us deeply about Himself, and about us. So we look at each one and see God's love and grace. They are like arrows in my hand, giving me strength to face my enemies, my idols, like worldly success, self-reliance, and pride.

I thought that pregnancy for Jaye at 36 years old with CF and diabetes would be devastatingly hard. But it was an easy pregnancy. Before we found out she was pregnant, Jaye was healthier than she has ever been. God truly sustained her and prepared her. I remember what my little Peruvian teller friend told me: "Children are a blessing. God will give you what you need. Don't worry."

We are in the throes once again of late nights and diapers. And it is wonderful. We spend hours each day oogling at Grace, getting her to giggle and smile.

And when she does, it's like nothing else.

Raising children is hard, especially when I think that I am responsible to shepherd them, to be their "pastor," And with little Grace I am praying that I can really get it right after all my practice on the other three.

I want to be a godly father to my brood. I don't want to get sucked into the success-driven mindset with my kids. It's so easy, for some reason. I've found in myself that although I work hard at choosing to forsake the success-crazy culture, I have occasional pangs of desire to see my kids succeed in sports, or academics, or even to achieve general social "coolness," whatever that is. But I know society works hard enough to teach that; I certainly don't need to help it.

Jaye and I have tried to downplay success, or winning, at anything that isn't directly related to following Jesus. It's fun if Colson wins a baseball game, or if Carter wins her gymnastics meet, or if Ayden wins her track race. We have fun as they are having fun. But we try to stress success in showing the fruit of the Spirit over anything else. We look for opportunities to celebrate how their faith is producing love or joy, self-control, or kindness. When I blow it with my kids and yell out of frustration, or when I fail to follow through with something I said I would do with or for them, I try to show them the need we all have for forgiveness, me especially, and to talk through how we are really feeling, both good and bad. We are trying to teach them that it is important to do your best in school, or in sports, or in music.

But in the end when they are grown, if they are successful fruit-bearers in the Kingdom, I really don't care how much money they make, what titles they bear, or what kind of a house they live in.

I'm in it for a different reason entirely.

TWELVE
MIRRORS

When Jaye and I decided to sell our house and move to Florida, we did it knowing that our good, no *great*, friends Jeff and Cami were there, and they were committed to us and we were committed to them.

One of the key lessons I learned through the twins' pregnancy and the birth of Colson was that I am not strong enough to make it on my own. God had given me a real challenge to my faith, and He brought me through it with a stronger dependence on Him, with the help of faithful people in our lives. But I realized something else through that experience. I realized that it wasn't just in hard times, times of suffering, that I needed the help of other people, but rather it was *all* the time. I found the definition of real success, but I realized how very hard it is to achieve.

I believe that the hardest thing in the world to do is to truly love another person with a self-sacrificing, self-denying, others-focused love, the kind of love Jesus had for his friends. This is exactly what Jesus called us to, and what His apostles called us to in their letters.

When Jesus stripped down as a servant, got on his knees, and cleaned the disciples nasty, dirty feet, He was demonstrating the love that we should have for one another, the love that we *must* have for one another if we are going to be called His followers. When He was done showing them this practical demonstration of love, he said, "Just as I have loved you, so you are to love one another." Why did he do this?

111

Why cleaning dirty feet? Couldn't He have just said, "Just as I am going to love you by dying on the cross as payment for your sin-debt to the Father, so you are to love one another"?

Yes, He could have. But He didn't.

Jesus chose to show us what love should look like between us in a seriously practical way. I mean, how often are you going to be presented in your life with the opportunity to die for your friends? Not often, or ever. But guess how often you have the opportunity to serve your spouse, your friends, your neighbors, and strangers in simple and practical ways? Every day. In a thousand ways.

How many of us men have said that we would die for our wives and children? But how often do we "clean their feet" on a daily basis, and not just on Christmas, Valentines Day and Easter?

When I first came to know Jesus, I was so grateful for God rescuing me from the darkness of the pit. With God's help in slowly pulling off the blinders, I started seeing how many of my daily activities were focused on fulfilling my desires, to do what I wanted to do, to bring myself satisfaction. I began to see, over time, that I walked around deceiving myself *about* myself at every turn, telling myself that I was good and better than most. I compared myself to other people and no matter what, I always found someone who made me feel better about myself.

But the fact is there is only one standard. Jesus. He is the only one that is good. And God desires my character, my thoughts, my actions, and my words to reflect him to the watching world. Not to attempt to act like him, but rather to *be* like him. I can never be perfect as he was, but I can, little by little, become more like him each day. And that takes effort. Effort to stay close to him so that he'll rub off on me. And I cannot possibly do that on my own, without the honest care of real friends.

Through college, I had roommates and housemates, all good guys who followed Christ. We had to share bathrooms and kitchens, pots and pans, parking spaces. That was a real challenge in learning how to live with people, but I didn't give away any of my autonomy to my roommates. I was still able to do what I wanted to do. I just had to work around the schedules of a couple of other guys and clean the bathroom when it was my turn.

But when I got married is when I started realizing that I was basically a selfish person. There we were, living side-by-side, sharing a bed, bedroom, a bathroom sink, a shower, our money, a car. It was no longer *my* stuff. It was now *our* stuff. But that was great to me. I truly loved sharing everything with my wonderful wife. What was hard was not *doing* what I wanted to do all the time.

Then Carter was born.

And *then* I realized how selfish I was.

This little baby was completely reliant upon us for everything. If I was watching a show, reading a book, or sleeping, and the baby needed to eat, burp, pee or poop, we had to take care of it. Suddenly, my autonomy was further eroded. But the baby grew, started walking, and then was *potty trained*. Ah, some of my autonomy was coming back. Then we had twins.

And only *then* did I realize how selfish I *still* was.

Carter was now 2.5 and learning how to do things for herself, although she still obviously needed a lot of attention. But now we had 2 babies and a 2.5 year old. Twice the bottles, twice the crying, and twice the poop. My autonomy was gone. But they were my children, my offspring, and my natural instincts of protecting your own kicked in. This was a time of reflection on my heart and how I must die to myself to give to my family. But that is a natural thing. A lot of my innate selfishness was eroding. I thought it was almost completely gone.

That's what I *thought*.

When we decided to move to Florida to reunite with Jeff and Cami, we wanted to live near each other so our kids could get together easily, realizing that even being a few houses away would not accomplish what we wanted: to live in community. Our friendship as couples was deep and abiding, and we loved hanging out with each other. Our kids had fun together, and we had seen how they grow in character by being with each other better than being alone. We wanted to experience what it means to live in real community.

So we decided to take the radical step of living next door to each other, side-by-side, sharing our back yards. We weren't going to accept halfway. It was all the way, baby.

You see, it's one thing to get married. It's another to have children. And it's still another to learn to deal with your selfishness in caring for your entire family. But when you live next door to someone else's family, whose kids are in and out of your house all day long, whose dog poops in your yard, who you see on a regular basis because you are eating together twice a week, it's an all-together different thing. When your child is crying because he fell down and got hurt, you console him without delay. But when another person's child falls down and starts crying, you might console, but there is a slight delay. "Should I help little Johnny? I helped him yesterday, should I do it again? Where's his mother anyway?" And that instantaneous calculation stems from your lack of desire to do more than you have to do.

If another family needs something, it's not a given that we react to help meet that need, because they aren't "our responsibility." In community, that family becomes your responsibility. You make a kind of a covenant to live and grow together. Your selfishness comes out loud and clear, if you are listening and have your eyes open to yourself.

We can live in isolation even in our own families, even though we are active in a church. There are countless people I have known who appear engaged in the lives of others, but in reality are emotionally removed from their spouses, their children, their "friends," and their coworkers. I think there are different reasons for this.

One is that we are ashamed of what is in our hearts and we've constructed facades to protect and create an image. We may feel better about maintaining that facade so we don't let anyone behind it to see how broken and messed up we are. And after a while, we begin to believe that the facade is the real us. And then we never have to admit our brokenness, or ask God for forgiveness and power to change, to become authentic people under the grace of God.

Another reason is we don't want to bear others' burdens. If we go deep, then we're going to hear about their struggles and pains. And that makes us responsible. We'll have to struggle with them, to pray with them, and to help them. And if we are responsible for another person then that is going to expose the fact that we don't really want to help them. We're too busy with our own struggles to want to help someone else. But that's exactly what we're called to do.

And there are other reasons as well. But when you're living right next door to your great friends, all of that goes out the window.

What I've found is that living in community, real intentional community, is like a mirror God uses to expose those things in ourselves that need work. Such close community helps us see those areas in our lives, the things we say, think, and do, that are not like Jesus. And it applies good *pressure* to get you ready to open yourself to the truth—about yourself.

Living in such close proximity brings almost daily opportunities to face who we really are.

Not long after we moved into our house in Atlanta, Jeff and Cami's third child, Lexi, was playing in Ayden's room. Lexi thought Ayden's bed would be the perfect place to open a fresh bottle of nail polish, the contents of which spilled out all over her new favorite bedspread, which brought Ayden, devastated and crying, to report the crime.

My instinctive reaction was to show Ayden I was there for her, to protect her interests. And Lexi knew better than to play with nail polish, let alone on the bed. This had to be dealt with.

This kind of unimportant issue has the potential to scar shallow friendships, and I've seen minor infractions between friends or their children ruin relationships. It's next to impossible to live like we do and not tick each other off on occasion. But relationships can't survive unless we choose to extend grace, mercy, and forgiveness to each other, over and over again.

And that's hard. Because who wants to die to themselves? It's not my inclination. But it's where my heart of hearts is, because that's the place Jesus inhabits in me. It's hard, but it's worth it. Jeff, Cami, and Jaye would also tell you that we're all better people because of it. And since God is in the business of making us better today than we were yesterday, I'd say our friendship is a great tool in His hands for each of us.

My first reaction passed and a better one took its place, one guided by the Holy Spirit. I realized I'm not to nurture and protect Ayden only, but Lexi as well. That's part of the deal; to love one another. So we hugged Lexi and she cried crocodile tears when she realized her mistake. But the conversation turned to forgiveness and love. We talked to Cami about the incident, and considered the splotch a great new addition to the character of the quilt.

Real community is a risk. We risk finding out that we don't want to turn away from selfishness, that we would rather just keep living to fill our appetites. We risk exposing our own sin and others rejecting us because of it. We risk giving more than the others and feeling like we're being taken advantage of, or worse, finding out that we abuse our friends' generosity. We risk being disappointed by our friends who don't show up when we think they should be there because they're not perfect and they can't read our minds.

We know we're not perfect, but when your friends don't meet your expectations, it's very inconvenient. It's worth it to find this out, though, to learn to serve, not to *be* served. And to learn to give and not expect parity.

It all sounds like an uncomfortable struggle, being forced to face innate selfishness all the time, and having to forgive and forgive. It is a struggle, maybe *the* struggle. But the struggle pales in comparison to the beauty.

And let me tell you, it is wonderfully beautiful.

We share weekly meals together. We built a patio adjoining our backyards, and we cut each others' grass, watch each others' kids, and spend hours upon hours talking. It's our commune-in-the-cul-de-sac without the hats, dresses, and overalls.

We need our friends. Although God has truly preserved Jaye's health over the years, she still suffers from acute illness at times because of her cystic fibrosis. Bacterial lung infections flare up causing her to feel absolutely miserable, her cough to be so heavy it seems unbearable, and she requires intravenous antibiotics for weeks. Every time Jaye gets sick, Cami automatically prepares double the food and calls us all over for dinner. Over the past 10 years I can't remember ever asking Cami for the help she's given us, for the countless meals she made. Or for the many, many times she has called to tell me that it was time to take Jaye out on a date and she would watch our kids. She just does it, without asking for anything in return. It's a picture of Jesus to us which we may not have seen without living in community.

Community is God's design. All of the friendships that I have experienced that are deep and abiding have come about in the Church, the body of Christ. It might be tempting to think that we don't need the organization called the church, that if we have real community with people that the organization isn't that important. In my experience, the only real community we can have comes in the context of the church.

There are countless books that speak to the importance, biblical authority, mission, and necessity of the church, so I won't attempt to share about that here. I can only say that a person's success in the Kingdom is always in the context of a church body, where people intentionally come together under authority, hear God's word regularly, and share with one another.

It is only in the context of the churches I have been involved in that God has given me the power to fight the battles of life. Our deep and eternal friendship with Joel and Teresa came through the church, as did our friendship with Jeff and Cami and Matthias and Lindsay.

I have to say, however, that there have been serious struggles in my life that came about *inside* the church. In fact, some of the most difficult and heart-wrenching conflicts in my life came about with leaders of the church who made *really* bad decisions.

When I arrived in the Kingdom I had this notion that the church is Heaven on earth. It wasn't a conscious notion, but my expectations were seriously high, especially of pastors. I put my pastors on pedestals where there was nowhere to go but down. I understood, even then, the common depravity of man, but in practice I thought some pastors were exceptionally spiritual and nearly immune to falling.

When I started seeing with my own eyes that my pastors had real weaknesses and sin, it was devastating. God used those times to shape me in profound ways, and to see that only God is good.

We, including pastors, are fallen people, in need of grace, on a daily basis. I still hold my pastors in high regard because they have a tough task in shepherding us sheep, especially the ones who put them on pedestals. But I don't expect them to be perfect, and so I can authentically pray for them now.

I believe no matter what problems we have with the organization, the church is the bride of Jesus, in need of constant help like me. And the mirrors we need in our lives come through His bride.

We need mirrors. You need friends who know you beyond the small talk we've all perfected to ward off the important probing questions. Only a very small percentage of people have the self-awareness and humility necessary for honest self-appraisal. I know I don't have it. We need others who will allow us to be close to them so we can get into each others' stuff and peel back the onion of our hearts, the layer after layer of selfishness, resentment, lack of forgiveness, and ego. We need to put ourselves in situations where the mirror is square in front of our noses, even if we don't like it.

When we started out in Florida it was an almost complete leap of faith. I knew that it was good and that God would provide, but that truth hadn't quite made it down deep into my heart yet. I hadn't yet learned *how* to trust on a daily basis. As was our regular, if not weekly, habit, Jeff and I spent many nights out on the back porch with music and beer. There were many times that I got scared and insecure about what I was doing and Jeff reminded me of God's faithfulness and His promises, and I would go to bed assured again and with greater faith.

There have been many times over the years that Jeff has shared his struggles with me and I've pointed out the truth that was hard for him to see in the midst of the problems, and he walked away with greater peace and faith. And he has done the same for me. That kind of thing wouldn't have happened if we weren't seriously in each other's lives on a regular basis. We need to be sharpened and we can't perform that necessary task on ourselves; it needs to be done by our community, our friends.

And I can tell you this: The word of God in the hands of a faithful friend is a wonderful teacher.

THIRTEEN
TRAGEDY

I just watched one of my favorite movies, *Revolutionary Road*. As far as I can tell it isn't a movie most people have seen. It should be a movie that everyone in America would have some knowledge of because of the star power it garnered with Leonardo DiCaprio and Kate Winslett, reuniting after their *Titanic* affair. Among movie critics, it's a movie that won considerable attention, but it wasn't well known by the general public until it was nominated for a few Academy Awards. The critics were all over the board, almost to the point that it seems like they were watching different movies.

Frank Wheeler, a 30-year-old, cubicle-sitting, corporate cog lives a typical middle-class life with his wife, April, and their two young kids. Frank puts on his suit every day and plunges into the office to do his thing while April stays at home with the kids, occasionally entertaining a neighbor over coffee talking about which flowers to plant in the yard. They get together with their neighbors for drinks and have some laughs, entertain guests for dinner on occasion, and that's how their lives tick on.

Frank and April represent a nice career and family situation that from the outside would be enviable by most.

But behind the seemingly normal, comfortable life of the Wheelers is a problem. It isn't a dark past sin, or a disease that threatens to rob them of their youth. The problem is, Frank and April get a glimpse of the truth. When they were first married, they thought of themselves as "special," not like the rest. They thought that they would evade the trappings of suburbia and live full lives of passion, accomplishing great things along the way. A few years later they come to the realization that their lives are stuck in a state of "hopeless emptiness," a phrase Frank uses to describe their lives.

If this movie is a realists' tragedy, then the couple's dinner guest John would be the muse, the truth-teller. He is a mentally disturbed patient at the hospital's psychiatric ward, but he speaks the truth. He tells Frank, "Now you've said it . . . Plenty of people are onto the emptiness, but it takes real guts to see the hopelessness."

Frank and April have realized that they are not special at all. They see that their life of going to work to make money to buy a nice house and a nice car, entertaining their nice friends and raising nice kids is a lie. It's pointless. Their minds are opened to reveal that theirs are empty lives. They look down the path they are on and see no hope, nothing to show for their lives and no real reason for them. Their passion, the fire inside, is slowly and effectively extinguished in the drab atmosphere of their comfort. They find no joy, and their marriage is suffering under the mundane.

Frank and April see the truth, and in a moment of clarity they decide to throw caution to the wind and move to Paris, a place they've always wanted to live. Frank is going to take time in Paris to find his true vocation, his true calling, and forsake the routine, comfortable life. They don't know how they will live or pay the bills, but they are following their dream. Immediately, their marriage is flooded with passion and you can feel the happiness, the *joie de vivre*. It's as if they come to life on the screen.

This movie is beginning to look like a typical American film with a nice, happy ending. But this movie is a tragedy. They don't go to Paris. Frank is offered a respectable promotion at work with a sizable increase and he sees the security that will bring to his family. Frank envisions the career path and sees himself as an insider. He realizes without ever admitting it that he is more secure, more comfortable with the career and family situation that he hates than the dream he loves. The hopeless emptiness may be drudgery, but it is a lot more comfortable, a lot more secure, and a lot easier.

Immediately their marriage reverts back to the incessant fighting, only now it is immensely compounded. They had their chance to live, but because of Frank they had to settle back into the lie, the facade. And it ends badly, very badly.

This movie did relatively poorly in the United States, but did very well abroad. Why is that? Is it because we Americans don't want to be confronted with this type of message-bearing tragedy? Americans love a happy ending. Don't get me wrong, I love a happy ending. But *Revolutionary Road* is not meant to simply entertain. It is meant to give us a glimpse. It's a message we need to hear. I know I need to hear it.

The inference of the movie is that had Frank and April been blind to the hopeless emptiness they probably would have been relatively happy, normal people. But they would be living a lie. And their lives, no matter how comfortable and secure would be rendered empty and without hope.

Why is that a message for us? Is there a vast epidemic of "hopeless emptiness" in our culture?

I think so. But that begs the question: What is it to live an empty life? What is it to live without hope? Is living in suburbia, going to work in a cubicle, entertaining your friends, and watching football on weekends an empty life? And is living in Paris living a full life?

Jesus said this, "I have come that they (you) may have life, and have it to the full" (John 10:10). And, "He who abides in me and I in him, he will bear much fruit. Apart from me you can do nothing." A fruitful, full life is one lived by following Jesus. Following Jesus is the most radical thing on earth. But it doesn't necessarily mean that life in suburbia is empty. And it doesn't necessarily mean that life in a foreign city is full. We don't need to move into a commune or become Amish to live a radical life in the Kingdom of God. Jesus taught me that following Him means seeking Him in every facet of my life and surrendering everything to what He wants me to do.

It is believing that if I trust Him He will literally show me what decisions to make.

It is obeying Him, wherever He may take me.

It is trusting Him for what my family and I need to survive and giving up on trusting in what is comfortable and secure.

It is living in real community with other people.

And it is reaching out to people stuck in the mire of hopeless emptiness to show them what God, by His grace, has shown me. That He loves me, forgives me, saves me, and because of that one day I will see Him face to face, and He will welcome me home to Heaven, forever, and ever, and ever, and ever. That is hope.

I love the Spanish word for hope—esperanza—which comes from the verb *esperar*, "to wait." So esperanza means "that for which we wait." In English it has come to connote the thing we really wish to happen but probably won't. Hope isn't what we wish for, it is what we know will happen and are simply waiting for.

When God first brought me face to face with the cross of Jesus, I saw clearly that I was living in a state of hopelessness and emptiness. But He brought me over from death to life. It was only later that I realized that comfort and security were idols of mine, like little statues that I worshiped secretly. God rescued me from trying to worship two Gods and I can honestly say now that I feel the blood running through my veins, and life is full. But that isn't the thrill of risk. It is God's Spirit working in me growing fruit. And it's fruit that will last, forever. Like a treasure chest in Heaven.

There are times when I doubt myself and ask if I made the right decision in leaving the career behind. It's usually when I experience a setback in my business and money is tight that I sense the seeds of doubt nestling into my heart. My mind then wanders to the nice office, the paycheck, and the beautiful house. And I wonder. What would my life be like had I stayed? And then it occurs to me that I just erased in my mind all the things that I now treasure the most. The things that God has done in me and the closeness I feel with Him, the freedom to serve, and the richness of faith.

God gave me an opportunity, an open door, and the vision to see a life that I never dreamed possible. And I walked through the door, by His grace. I know that had I not taken the step life would have gone on. But I would have continued to longingly ponder what it must be like to really believe the promises of God. Mine looks like a very average life, and maybe even foolish. But I wouldn't trade any of the hard times of learning to live by faith and experiencing God provide for my secure and prestigious but worry-filled life of before.

FOURTEEN
MEDIOCRE

"Mediocre" is such an ugly word in our American vocabulary.

Do you have any of those "Quotes to Live By" books of inspirational slogans? If so, you've probably read some quotes about mediocrity and how vile it is.

"We must overcome the notion that we must be regular. It robs you of the chance to be extraordinary and leads you to the mediocre." (Uta Hagen). Being mediocre is something to be disdained and shunned and to be treated like cancer, and certainly not something to be pursued. Of course, mediocrity is going to be thrust upon the masses, but it is never something that you should aspire to, or so goes the thinking.

I look back over my life so far and I can see a series of forks in the road where I had to make a decision. The decisions were between what was best for my reputation and comfort, and what was truly and eternally best for me.

Going to the relatively unknown college was my first big decision into mediocrity. I wasn't exactly sure I had made the right decision when everyone around me, except my immediate family, seemed perplexed and disappointed. When almost everyone's thinking is opposite yours, it tends to make you question your sanity.

When I fell in love with Jaye I knew that choosing that college was a good decision. Years later we made the big decision to sell our McMansion and leave my cushy career behind and venture off into a life of self-employment and real community. That was my second big decision into mediocrity.

This road has often been very challenging, requiring a great deal of effort on God's part to remind me to trust Him in all things with my *whole* heart, to put my faith in Him to provide for us and sustain us. I look back at who I was and see that I believed strongly in Jesus as Savior of the world (and even me), but I didn't practically believe the idea of God as my Father and Provider.

God has been chipping away at me to get rid of my practical atheism, believing that His Word is true about how to be saved, but not practically and literally believing the rest about how He will give us what we need, that I can cast all my cares on Him because He (literally) cares for me.

God led Jaye and I down a road where we have to truly depend on Him for our needs, where we are in intentional community with people, and where we have the best opportunities to love God and love people we have ever experienced. Without a doubt in my mind, stepping off the ladder of success in the world and into mediocrity in the world's eyes has been the most rewarding, faith building, fruitful experience of my life. This life of *unsucceeding* in the world's eyes has given me the best chance to be able to serve my wife daily, be with my children, serve my church, meet with men in need, and help my friends.

I am very far from being the fruitful man I want to be. And I'm far from being like Jesus in loving people. But I am much farther down the road now than I ever was before. The pressures for success at work I succumbed to before along with the self-imposed pressures to succeed are now gone, and we rely on God to give us our daily bread. Although I had a consistent paycheck from a reliable company before and have zero consistency in income now, I have more peace trusting that God is our provider than I ever did before. And that is more valuable than a 401k, pension, or a paycheck every Friday.

Every 6 months or so, once in the summer and every Christmastime, Jaye and I watch the movies *It's a Wonderful Life* and *Family Man*. It's *a Wonderful Life* is a classic that everyone has seen and knows. *Family Man* is the modern day version except the plot line is backwards.

In *It's a Wonderful Life* the main character, George Bailey, is thwarted at every turn by life's circumstances in his pursuit of success and ends up being a failure in the world's eyes, only to find out through a vision given by an angel that he is truly rich because of the love he has in his life.

Family Man is the story of Jack Campbell, an incredibly wealthy, young, single, president of a merger and acquisitions firm, who is given a vision by an angel of what his life would have been like had he married his college sweetheart instead of pursuing his career. He goes to bed alone one night in his swanky Upper Manhattan penthouse condo with his Ferrari sports car valet parked outside and wakes up in a 4 bedroom, 2.5 bath suburban New Jersey average house with his wife, 2 kids, slobbering dog, and 8 year old minivan in the driveway.

The story is about his progression from true disdain for the mediocre life he is stuck in to true love for the family life with his wife and kids. In the end, the angel appears again and tells him the vision is coming to an end, but Jack doesn't want to go back. He realizes that the average, mediocre life of a car tire salesman with a wife and kids who love him and whom he loves is infinitely more valuable and desirable than the solitary life with the Ferrari and the penthouse.

I watch those movies every year because I am fickle. I forget. I really want to radically pursue true success in God's economy and trust Him for everything else I need. I just need to be reminded that true success cannot be balanced with the false kind the world values.

My life choices have never presented such stark contrasts as Ferraris and minivans. But the point is the same, it's only a matter of degree. I now see that either I am pursuing success in the Kingdom of God and everything else, including my vocation, as a means to that end, or I'm not. Jesus was clear and didn't parse his words. I need to be equally clear with myself and be sure that I never justify a desire for wealth and/or prestige by claiming to be doing the best for my family.

I've gone back and forth over the years about how I feel about wealth. The Bible is full of wealthy people doing good things, and it's full of wealthy people doing awful things. I've read over and over again about how it's easier for a camel to go through the eye of a needle than a rich man to enter the Kingdom of God, and that the love of money is the root of all sorts of evil. I know really godly rich people who really do love God and trust Him for their lives and give not out of guilt for being filthy rich, but because they love to be generous. I see that God may rain down money on some people as a result of some skill or invention they have, and that is wonderful, so long as they use it for His glory. What seems clear to me now, and seems to get clearer all the time, is that setting my heart on striving for wealth and prestige in this world will always lead to fruitlessness in the Kingdom.

When I started making money in my career, and having to make financial decisions for my family, I began to intently read Jesus' parable of the soils. I've always loved Jesus' clarity that there are two kinds of people, those who follow him, and those who don't. The sheep and the goats. The believers and the unbelievers. But when I read this parable, over and over again, I couldn't grasp it.

And it terrified me.

He said that the Gospel is like a seed that falls on different kinds of soil, which represent the different ways people respond to it. The first soil always made sense to me: Some of the seed falls along the path where the farmer carrying it is walking, and the birds quickly come and eat it up. That's the guy who hears the Gospel and rejects it outright. That is most of the world. That always made perfect sense to me. It was black and white.

It was the next two that scared me. The farmer throws some seed on some rocky places, but because there wasn't much soil, the plant sprang up quickly. But when the sun came out the plant was scorched and died quickly because it didn't have any root.

The third kind of soil seems perfectly fine. The seed falls, and the plant grows. It has good roots and seems perfectly fine as a plant goes.

But over time, thorn bushes grow up around it. The plant doesn't die, it just doesn't produce any grain. It's what the farmer does with this plant that makes it scary.

Jesus got with his 12 closest friends, His disciples, and explained the soil scenarios. He said that the second is the person who accepts the gospel with "joy", but they have no root "in themselves." And He said that when "tribulation or persecution arises on account of the word" they quickly fall away. I grasped this scenario.

But then I started thinking about myself as the average Christian in America. I don't face tribulation or persecution because of the Gospel. Not only that, I can hardly imagine tribulation or persecution happening in the United States because of our faith. Sure, we might be made to feel "strange" because of what we believe, or our church's steeple might get rejected by the zoning board, but is that the kind of tribulation or persecution that Jesus was talking about? I thought about a life of going to church, volunteering with the youth ministry, going to Sunday school, maybe even being an elder or deacon, but never experiencing tribulation or persecution because of my faith, and so never being tested to know if I really believed.

"Does that happen?" I wondered. "Could that be me?"

When the twins came, my faith was tested. And I came through it believing God. It wasn't persecution, but it was tribulation. The suffering I experienced was initially because of my circumstances, but it became suffering because I doubted my faith and where my trust lied. God brought me through it.

My real dilemma was with the third soil. Jesus explained that "the worries of this life, the deceitfulness of wealth and the desires for other things come in and choke the word, making it unfruitful."

My life as a Christian to this point had been checkered with worry about my life, spending a lot of energy and time focused on accumulating money and thinking about what I could do with it. I spent a lot of time at church and doing church things, but I knew that this soil described my heart, for at least a large part of my time. There were many times I was focused on being fruitful and serving, but a lot of time was focused on the cares of this life and money too. How could I know if this described me?

I read more and more of what Scripture says about following Jesus, and He made it clear that you know a true Jesus-follower by the character of his or her life like you know a tree by it's fruit.

The house I grew up in was built on an old apple farm with many different kinds of apple trees. In the winter I couldn't ever remember which tree was the golden-delicious, and which were the red-delicious. It was only when I saw the apples form that I could distinguish the two. At this point in my life I didn't know if I had been truly fruitful. Were love, joy, peace, patience, kindness, gentleness, goodness, faithfulness, and self-control what marked my life? Or did I just know a lot of the right answers and go to the right church? And did any of the Christians around me really even know what to look for to distinguish a fruitful person from a good but unfruitful person?

When God led me to give up the career, sell the house, and begin a life of really believing Him, I did want to give up setting my heart on building wealth in the name of security. It was later on that I came to another dilemma. I realized that I can give up striving for success as defined by money, but I can still want prestige, or respect from others, more than God's way. I can live free of the desire for money but still desire to be liked, respected, even revered, by other people.

At the core it was the same desire.

I've had countless conversations with people where my aim was not the glory of God, but building a better opinion of myself in their minds. Here again I saw that someone may be the most respected person in their field because God has blessed them. But I have also seen in myself and countless other people a desire to be respected, to be thought highly of, and that desire is a desire for success in this world.

There was a time as a Christian when I didn't really believe God loved me and I looked for affirmation, affection, and assurance from people to feel better. When I don't really believe God loves me, I manipulate to gain acceptance in church-wide emails, I speak spiritual words of wisdom to tickle the ears of listeners, I want religious titles to feel respectable, I want biblical authority over others to feel important.

But when I *know* that God loves me I can authentically love people, as I am, as they are. When I *really* believe that God has declared me, once and for all, accepted as His loved child then I don't need to speak, I can listen and hear people. I don't have to impress anyone. I can let people win arguments and not prove myself. I can forgive. I am free to not care if people like me or not. I can put aside the cardboard facade me and let people see who I really am behind the false walls of respectability. And I can see past their facades and love them anyway.

When I desire it in my heart, prestige becomes a cold iron chain to my flesh that binds me. It's the prestige that comes with being wise, godly, spiritual, or full of knowledge that is particularly dangerous. That's the kind that can make me think I really am special.

No, I don't want prestige. At least I don't want to want it. Really believing God, trusting Him, that He loves me and has made me a permanently new creation, is the key to loose the chains.

God is opening my eyes more and more as I walk down this road to see that the amount of money I make or don't make, my position in any organization, top or bottom, or my ranking in any field, good or bad, is of no consequence. What matters is the bent of my heart and mind. If my heart is set on success in this world then it cannot be set on success in the Kingdom of God. Because, according to Jesus, where your heart is so is your treasure.

God doesn't call us to be successful in the world and mediocre in His Kingdom. He calls us to be successful in His Kingdom, even if it requires you to be mediocre in the world. He doesn't call us to be mediocre to Him. He has taught me, and year after year He continues to teach me, that if I try to be successful in this world by striving for wealth or respect, then I end up being fairly fruitless in His Kingdom.

God wants us to be successful, to prosper, in loving Him and people, first and foremost, experiencing real joy by knowing Him deeply, and in trusting him with real, radical faith. That is success, and the only success that matters.

If God gives us success and money then we should say, "Amen" and receive it, and use it doubly for His purposes. But if our feet are running the race for money or prestige, then it is better to lose.

It sounds so counter intuitive, but could mediocrity as the world defines it actually be something to aspire to? I'm given the freedom to decide each day which definition to accept.

There are two roads. One is successful living in God's Kingdom. And the other is success in this world. It's not two roads converged into one. It is a fork in the road that I'm faced with every day. It's impossible to authentically live on both. And with my Father, my Lord, and my Counselor helping I can choose the road that leads to real life.

EPILOGUE

One night, God gave me a children's story to help me remind my kids that if any good comes from their lives, it's because of God's grace and His work, because He is the only one that is good. But when I had written it, it occurred to me that I am a child. My Father had stripped me of many of the things in my heart I felt made me strong and independent, and He lovingly made me realize I am weak without Him. I too depend on Him as a child depends on his father.

Jesus said, "Anyone who will not receive the Kingdom of God like a little child will never enter it." (Luke 18:17).

God gave me this story to help me remember that fruit is only good in my life if it is being used by Him to nourish and refresh the people around me. I thought it was for my kids. But it was for me too, as His child.

GRAPES

Once there was a vine that had many branches.

On the branches grew big and bubbly grapes. One of the branches was bigger and more beautiful than the rest. And the grapes he grew were bigger and bubblier than any others.

Now nearby a little girl lived in a small house and didn't have much of anything. And she loved to come to the vine and pick bubbly purple grapes.

One day, when the girl was hungry, she came to the vine and saw the branch that was bigger and more beautiful than all the rest. He had big and bubbly grapes.

"My, what pretty purple grapes," the girl said.

"Oh, I hope she will take my grapes," the branch thought. "Then she won't be hungry any more."

The girl did eat as many of the grapes from the branch as she could, and she went home that night with a full, happy tummy.

The branch thought to himself, "I'm so glad my grapes made the girl's tummy happy. Now she isn't hungry any more."

Well, the next day the girl was hungry again. So she came back to the vine.

She found the branch and his big and bubbly grapes and ate as many as she could. And she returned for home again with a big, full, happy tummy.

The branch was so happy. "She ate my grapes again!" he said. "My grapes made her tummy happy!"

Well, after that, the branch looked around and said to himself, "The girl eats my grapes because mine are the biggest and bubbliest! I should be higher on the fence so I can get more sun, instead of being down here mixed in with all the other branches."

So the branch stretched as far as he could to the higher part of the fence above all the other branches.

And the next day, when the girl came, she noticed the big, beautiful branch right away. "Right here," the branch said to himself. "Here I am!" The girl ate all the grapes she could from the big branch until her tummy was full once again.

The branch was so excited he could barely contain himself. "She only picked *my* grapes again! I really *am* special!

She probably doesn't eat from the other branches because my grapes are the best. I should be even higher or the other branches might make my grapes small and squishy like theirs."

So the branch looked up and saw he could go higher on the fence, right to the tippy top. So he stretched and stretched, but he couldn't reach. His grapes weighed him down.

"If I shake off some of my grapes then I'll be able to reach."

So the branch shook and shook until most of his grapes fell off.

But he still couldn't reach any higher. He thought, "Maybe if I shake off just a few more."

So he shook and he shook. And pretty soon, all his grapes fell off. And all his leaves as well.

But the branch didn't notice. He gathered up all his strength and he stretched and stretched and after that he stretched a little bit more. Until . . .

He made it! He made it to the top of the fence..

"Now I'll make the best bubbly grapes ever!"

The next day, the girl came, but when she saw the branch, she passed him by and ate from the other branches instead. The biggest branch was mystified. "Why didn't she take my grapes?" he asked the vine when she had gone back home with a full, happy tummy again.

"Because you don't have any grapes," the vine replied.

What? The branch looked and saw it was true. "What happened to my grapes?" he asked in horror.

"You broke off from me," said the vine.

"No, I didn't," the branch whined.

"You wanted to be higher than the other branches," said the vine.

And then the branch remembered: the *vine* made his grapes the biggest and the bubbliest. It wasn't him at all. He forgot that the vine had put him at just the right spot to make his grapes. And he forgot that without being in the vine he couldn't make any grapes at all.

The branch drooped. But just before he turned brown, the vine reached up to him and grabbed him right in the spot where he broke off.

"OW!" the branch screamed and it hurt more than anything. But the branch didn't complain.

Soon he was growing again, like a brand new branch. And he grew and grew, and had big and bubbly purple grapes once again. The girl came back and ate his grapes and others' too until her tummy was full and happy.

And from that day on, the new branch stayed close to the vine. He shared his sunlight with the other branches. And he was very happy.

• • •

This little story helps me remember that I will never have this all figured out. There are times when I take inventory of myself and see reflections of God in my thoughts, in my character, and in my actions, and I feel my chest swell and my chin lift higher as pride fills my heart. Instead, I should be humbled that God would show up more clearly in my life, overcoming my love for myself. But that pride is a prickly shoot springing from me that God tenderly prunes away only to graft in more nourishing fruit. He is the vine. I am just a branch. He is the skillful gardener. I am His workmanship. He fills me with His loving kindness all the days of my life, and turns my dry heart into warm, tender ground, fertile and rich, ready to bear fruit.

This life of trusting God and forsaking worldly success is hard. In fact, it seems impossible. Everything seems stacked against us. But if we ask Him to, little by little, God will teach us to trust Him. He will show us in small, medium, and big ways how we can trust Him. He will chip away at those idols that we worship so that He is the only centerpiece of our lives.

Jesus said,

"I am the vine and you are the branches, he who abides in Me and I in him, he bears much fruit. For apart from me you can do nothing." (John 15:5)

God continues to teach me to abide in Him, to stay close to Jesus, and all that entails. Unfortunately, it isn't like a set of steps that once you reach a step you never have to revisit it. Abiding in Jesus is more like a circle. At least it is for me. I seem to come back to the same point I started at and He has to re-teach me the same lessons. But I never cease to be amazed that He does reveal Himself to me and in me, and when I am abiding in Him, he does bear fruit in me. It is tempting to feel proud of myself when He does, and to take credit for His goodness. But He loves me in that too, always reminding me that He is jealous for His glory, and that, as Jesus told the rich young ruler, "Only God is good."

I figure that I'm about half way through this life, if all goes well. As I look back on the path I've traveled it seems as though it has been a twisting road, not a simple one with straight lines from point A to point B. There were times early on when I thought I could chart my path, planning to avoid the pitfalls, steep hills, and thorns. But my plans never worked out; I always ended up far off from where I thought I would be.

The path has been rocky at times, where I stumbled, bled a little, sometimes a lot, and got back up stronger than before. It has been up and down, hard and easy. I've rested along quiet streams in shady meadows. I've had to all out sprint. And all along the way there were forks in the road where I had to make a decision about which way to go. They weren't decisions between good and evil, but in retrospect they were between pursuing what I wanted and pursing God's Kingdom. And I didn't know until now that the path has been a gradual climb up a mountain.

I can look back and see the beauty of the mountainside behind me, with the valley and streams and meadows below. All that I saw while walking was what was immediately before me, not the fascinating landscape in full view. Not being able to see what was around each twist of the road was before a source of anxiety. I've come to peace with not knowing what tomorrow brings, because I know that God is sovereign, good, and just, and He loves me as His child. *He* knows the future and He holds me in His hands. That's enough for me. I can't wait to get to the top of the mountain to meet my Father there, face to face. I already feel like I've seen Jesus face to face; after all, He is the one showing me the way, He is the light on the path. And He is going to get me home.

"Trust in the Lord with all your heart and lean not on your own understanding. In all your ways acknowledge Him and He shall direct your paths" (Proverbs 3:5-6).

ARE YOU AN UNSUCCEEDER?

Are you an unsucceeder too? Are you hearing a call to choose a simple, literal faith in the Provider of all your necessities?

Do you long for freedom from worry about money and the deceitfulness of wealth?

Have you experienced something you can no longer ignore?

If you're a guy who'd like to trust in something higher than success, money and prestige, we invite you to check out www.unsucceeding.net to connect with our community and share about your experience, your desires, your pains, and your hope. We want to hear how God is speaking to you, in your own voice.

Honestly, what guy doesn't need to experience a transformation of radical faith, love, and community?

A Note from the Editor

Don't you just love crazy stories?

One day, a couple of months after starting my little writing and editing community, I got a call from a guy asking for help with publishing his book—a book he apparently never intended to write, but somehow did.

Okay, I thought, *but how'd he find me?* Maybe he knew I used to be at a big publishing house. But did he know I was singing a new tune, one that doesn't quite square with promoting and selling books? How could he know *that?* I hadn't told anyone. I was too afraid of looking like a schmuck.

What we both found out was that we were both already in the same club and we were being set up to explore an idea too few guys seem to have really found yet. And for some reason, it seems to require looking like a schmuck.

My new tune is that authors need no fame or position to be publishable. They just need to be humble, exceptionally patient, and brave as badgers. Now that you've read Kyle's crazy story, you know he's all that and more.

Someone put us together. And I wouldn't be surprised if maybe you're thinking of someone he's got in mind to join the unsucceeder club too.

Mick Silva

Acknowledgments

I wish that everyone could know Jaye. For so many years I equated one's level of knowledge of God with their level of godliness. I thought that the more someone could articulate the truths of Scripture the more holy they were. Jaye isn't eloquent and doesn't pretend to be. She doesn't layer her prayers with SAT words and seminary catch phrases. And so I thought that she wasn't as spiritual as me.

A few years ago I was confronted with the truth that the height of holiness isn't the knowledge of God. The height of holiness is love; real 1 Corinthians 13 kind of love. Jaye loves me and all those around her better than anyone I know. Not only does she endure daily breathing treatments, medications, insulin pump mainte-nance, homeschooling our kids, exercise, and constant coughing, she has to endure me. And she has never complained, as long as I've known her, about her circumstances. She has never doubted God's plan. And she has never wavered in her faithfulness and love for me. It is truly miraculous. I love her so deeply and I thank God for her. She is my great example of what I hope to be like one day. She is my greatest blessing.

Thanks also to Cami Summers for reading through my midnight Jerry Maguire memo, as I called this, for that's all it was until it turned into something more. She gave me great pointers and encouragement to finish. May God bless Cami for blessing me.

Thanks to Jon Stamberg for the time and energy he gave to give great thoughts about this book.

Thanks to the uber-cool Steve Brown for taking the time to read this little book and actually endorsing it. His deep, deep voice is deep, but not as deep as his deep, deep love for Jesus.

And thanks go to Mick Silva for responding to a completely random email from a completely unknown person telling a story about jumping off the success ladder and landing in God's hands. He was willing to read, and re-read, and edit, and edit, and edit this thing so that the message came through clearly. He not only gave editing advice, he gave encouragement, which was so much more valuable to me, a clueless newbie. May God bless Mick richly for putting not just his skills and experience into this project, but his heart also.

Thanks for reading. May God bless you.

Kyle Drake